# PENETRALIA

# PENETRALIA

Clayton Eshleman

BLACK
WIDOW
PRESS

Boston, MA

Black Widow Press is an imprint of Commonwealth Books, Inc., Boston, MA. Distributed to the trade by NBN (National Book Network) throughout North America, Canada, and the U.K. All Black Widow Press books are printed on acid-free paper, and glued into bindings. Black Widow Press and its logo are registered trademarks of Commonwealth Books, Inc.

Joseph S. Phillips and Susan J. Wood, Ph.D., Publishers
www.blackwidowpress.com

Cover Art: Mary Heebner, CENOTE # 5, 1989, collage with pastel, pigment, and canvas on Stonehenge rag paper 50" x 28". www.maryheebner.com

Design & production: Kerrie L. Kemperman

ISBN-13: 978-0-9971725-8-4

Printed in the United States
10 9 8 7 6 5 4 3 2 1

# ACKNOWLEDGEMENTS

Some of these poems and the interview have appeared, occasionally in ear-lier forms, in the following periodicals and blogs: *Alligatorzine, International Times* (London), *New American Writing, Montevidayo, Black Tongue, House Organ, Brooklyn Rail, The Wolf* (England), *Poems And Poetics, Hambone, Denver Quarterly, The Black Herald* (Paris), *Jivin' Ladybug, Spoon River Poetry Review, Mantis, The Doris, Café Review, Shearsman* (England), *Truck, Hungarian Review* (Budapest), *X-Peri, Rain Taxi, Seedings, A Literary Journal Celebrating 30 Years of the San Luis Obispo Poetry Festival*, and *The Canary Islands Connection: Fifty-Nine Contempo-rary American Poets.*

"North Tower Exploding" appeared bilingually (French translation by Peter Cockelbergh) in *Le Mal now, Topographie de l'art*, Paris, 2013.

*Blaze VOX*, Buffalo, NY published "The Jointure" as a chapbook in 2012 and "Nested Dolls" (in a significantly different version) as a chapbook in 2013.

"At Eighty-One" was published in *Resist Much / Obey Little, Inaugural Poems to the Resistance*, Spuyten Duyvil Press, 2017.

Poems that have an asterisk to the far right of the title are briefly annotated in a Notes section at the end of the book.

# ALSO BY CLAYTON ESHLEMAN

## POETRY

Mexico & North [1962]

Indiana [1969]

Altars [1971]

Coils [1973]

The Gull Wall [1975]

What She Means [1978]

Hades in Manganese [1981]

Fracture [1983]

The Name Encanyoned River: Selected Poems 1960–1985 [1986]

Hotel Cro-Magnon [1989]

Under World Arrest [1994]

From Scratch [1998]

My Devotion [2004]

An Alchemist with One Eye on Fire [2006]

Reciprocal Distillations [2007]

The Grindstone of Rapport [2008]

An Anatomy of the Night [2011]

Clayton Eshleman / The Essential Poetry 1960–2015 [2015]

## PROSE

Antiphonal Swing: Selected Prose 1962–1987 [1989]

Companion Spider: Essays [2002]

Juniper Fuse: Upper Paleolithic Imagination & the Construction of
the Underworld [2003]

Archaic Design [2007]

The Price of Experience [2013]

## JOURNALS AND ANTHOLOGIES

Folio [Bloomington, Indiana, 3 issues, 1959–1960]

Quena [Lima, Peru, 1 issue, edited, then suppressed by the
North American Peruvian Cultural Institute, 1966]

*Caterpillar* [New York–Los Angeles, 20 issues, 1967–1973]

*A Caterpillar Anthology* [1971]

*Sulfur* [Pasadena–Los Angeles–Ypsilanti, 46 issues, 1981–2000]

*A Sulfur Anthology* [2015]

## TRANSLATIONS

*Pablo Neruda, Residence on Earth* [1962]

*César Vallejo, The Complete Posthumous Poetry*
(with José Rubia Barcia) [1978]

*Aimé Césaire, The Collected Poetry*
(with Annette Smith) [1983]

*Michel Deguy, Given Giving* [1984]

*Bernard Bador, Sea Urchin Harakiri* [1986]

*Conductors of the Pit: Major Works by Rimbaud, Vallejo, Césaire,
Artaud, & Holan* [1988, 2005]

*Aimé Césaire, Lyric & Narrative Poetry 1946–1982*
(with Annette Smith) [1990]

*César Vallejo, Trilce* [1992, 2000]

*Antonin Artaud, Watchfiends & Rack Screams*
(with Bernard Bador) [1995]

*Aimé Césaire, Notebook of a Return to the Native Land*
(with Annette Smith) [2001]

*César Vallejo, The Complete Poetry* [2007]

*Bernard Bador, Curdled Skulls* [2010]

*Bei Dao, Endure* (with Lucas Klein)[2011]

*Aimé Césaire, Solar Throat Slashed* (with A. James Arnold) [2011]

*Aimé Césaire, The Original 1939 Notebook of a Return to the Native Land*
(with A. James Arnold) [2013]

José Antonio Mazzotti, *Sakra Boccata* [2013]

## BOOKS ON CLAYTON ESHLEMAN

*Minding the Underworld: Clayton Eshleman & Late Postmodernism*, Paul Christensen [1991]

*Clayton Eshleman / The Whole Art*, Edited by Stuart Kendall [2014]

*For my wounded angel*

"The 'deep image' is the poetic image struggling with the darkness. The image rescued from the lie of the unthreatened. Not as a literary prescription, for writing better poems or nurturing the language, but from an impasse in the soul, in which the protective 'reality' & false emblems of the inherited past have drawn a blank. Not as a neurotic outcry either, from the weakness of a self-pity, but in the wholeness & fitness of the poet's vision."
                                                                            —Jerome Rothenberg


"The image must be twisted if, in making a renewed assault on the nervous system, it is to unlock the deeper sensations, the mysteries of accident and intuition."
                                                                            —Francis Bacon


"There is an intolerable aspect to every image, as image. Its habitation in the undersense of things is their underworld and 'death.' An image as a simulacrum is but a shadow of life and the death of concretistic faith. Imagining implies the death of the natural, organic view of life and this repels our common sense. Hence, the underworld stinks; dung and corpses; brimstone. Images are demonic, of the very devil; keep a distance. Have a keen nose."
                                                                            —James Hillman

# TABLE OF CONTENTS

# FOR CONNIE CULP  *

Reface me.
Deliver me from this shot gun blast mess.

A hole where had been the middle of her face.

22 hours for new blood vessels, hollow
white arteries, hair-dense stitches starting to pulse.

Donor face. Anna Kasper mask. Xipe wear.
Through the face of one dead the eyes of one living.

Will her soul reject her mask?

("You'll leave like a breeze," warns one tremble-anchored bush)

To breathe,   & to live,   behind the entropy of the mask.
To appear Other.  Not to be Other but to radiate
Other as a kind of starlit mire.
Face stadium through which the Anna Kasper specters flit.

Miracle for Connie Culp now able to walk down the street
without being stared at as a freak.

What might have been the first mask?

The eyes of one's dead rival staring through a waterfall?

# POSTHUMOUS MASK

This mask is in motion, acrawl with web building,
an eight-legged mile-stained mandala
dread cocked in its refusal to disclose synthesis.
Over us Caryl opens a black umbrella,
                              exciting bat sonorities.
Together we walk the Crocodile of the Earth
observing Her birth hole, out of which deer are streaming.
Spider is our red transformer.
Her nets gilded with rabbits & peccaries.
By stingray we are pressed to owl, by owl we are intact in ceiba.


My heart face undergoes *hinoki* to become a Noh mask for poetry:
image depth: inlet for the infinite
at anticline with the mystery of fetal curl,
a masque of larval shadows: Yorunomado's mind.


Chrysalis & rectitude of a life at rail
with the hammerhead knitted behind time,
with thinning boa surf,
with Pandora's hexagram, hex agonal with trances.


This mask is my memorial brass:
destiny's spored, diasporic double.

# A DAUGHTER LIFE

In this dream Nancy Dugan was my daughter—
lovely, blonde, we walked an English town
& I explained to her that I loved her
as my daughter, or just
her. I loved & thus
would not want to enmesh her in a threesome,
so sex was out, & she
would have to make her way
with & without me,
                    I kept fingering
the creative tenebrosity of books
as students watched.
One like a bird, with crimson purple foliage
feather pages, rich stirrings &
nestings...
                    What have I noticed in this life?
Impermanence vying eternally
with permanence    loses to the fantasy of
a daughter life, progeny of
the imagination, fulfillment
via the book, that possibility for
others to come
along the rough corduroy streets of
towns of the dream. I suppose Peter
Redgrove is there,    & maybe Zoe
is my daughter too. My parents,
when I was nine, discussed,
while driving back from Elkhart, the adoption of
a little girl. Excited me,
that I might soon not be
so alone. Never passed, & Nancy Dugan,
my age, raised by her single mother,
in an apartment on Meridian south of 34th Street,
became my vision of a sister.

I suppose I desired her & was afraid?
To make a move? She was Johnny
Wardlaw's girlfriend, before a fireplace,
cover of the *Indianapolis Star Supplement,*
1952. Time's entanglements
yield      & then to have seen Nancy
a decade ago at the Whitakers in
northside Indianapolis,
a smoking crone! I had asked that
she be invited, & here she is.
I sit before her as before a pyre of
my youth & any lingering
sentimentality over Indianapolis &
that 4705 dining room porthole window through which
slung between Cro-Magnon &
Bugs Bunny poles, I dreamed of discovering
under the GI screwing his girlfriend in the Butler Woods
a magical carrot, or
a chorus from Bud Powell.

# MANDALIZING *

Sunday, August 9, 2009, 11:11 AM

dear Anne, am unsure of what to make of angel as "witness." Tom Cheetham quotes Henry Corbin describing "the Self [as] the heavenly counterpart of a pair or a syzygy made up of a fallen angel, or an angel appointed to govern a body, and of an angel retaining his abode in heaven... This syzygy individualizes the Holy Spirit into an individual Spirit who is the celestial paredros of the human being, its guardian angel, guide, companion, helper and savior." Cheetham defines "fravarti" as heavenly spirit, a term that I find to be a shredding cloud. I think of soul as the power that animates imagination.

In Kyoto, 1963, I was discovering my own soul &, at the same time, the extent to which that soul was in exile. Via my work on Vallejo (while being stymied by Vallejo in translation), I constructed my own guide, Yorunomado, out of the name of the coffee shop where I translated in the afternoon (Yorunomado = Night Window), & a National Geographic photo of a Sepik Delta head hunter sitting on a reed bench looking at a skull (he had presumably taken) on a bench before him. I think that in Corbin terms, Yorunomado presented himself as a Spirit helper indicating to me the extent to which imagination might lead. He was also my own homemade construct of an angel. I was involved in a shamanic initiation (knowing nothing about shamanism at the time), in which was I to initiate myself off myself, & in the poem "The Book of Yorunomado," disembowel myself of the old "given" life Clayton, for a creative life under the aegis of this complex construct. So that is my background on this "combined object," one of my own making, a kind of rag & bone shop construct that over the years has kept me outside of any return to organized religion (I know you do not think of Buddhism as a religion, but I do, & I guess we have to agree to disagree on that one). Funny, I read your letter right before going to bed last night & decided to wait until tomorrow morning (this morning) to respond. Upon waking at 6:45 AM, the following lines presented themselves:

Self is an ever-shifting mobile of
masks linked to masks,
as if by rod-like umbilici,
masks that are shaped like windmill slats
going off "on their own," then regrouping in the assemblies that
Wifredo Lam envisioned as Personages
whose total make-up is "beyond."

Are these masks puppets on the strings of an angel puppeteer?
Do all the layers of "I" find resonance in an Angel of the Face?

The hardening of Christianity arteries.
A Mazdean vision now lost to Iranian ayatollahs.

The poet can have no system overseer, no
third eye at the peak of a pyramid like a search-light onto
   his psychic sleights—
his stare weighed stairway
   descends through
a Self-assembled sylphwork
      of anti-saviorial
         defiance.

Returning to your letter: I don't have the word "anthropocene" in my vo-
cabulary. How do you understand it? Does it mean something like: the
world as determined by man? If so, I think you are stuck with the Upper
Paleolithic as your base, or back wall, & the initial divisions between nature
& culture (Hans Peter Duerr is good here on the figure of the *hagazussa* in
flight on broom rocket as she crosses back & forth over her fence sitting
place between wilderness & proto-culture (see Duerr's *Dreamtime* if you
want more on this)).

   I am also fascinated by your "cool red star" again not having the term in
my vocabulary.

   Gary Snyder once wrote me that he had totally dismissed "soul" as a
counter until re-encountering it in the writings of James Hillman, where-
upon he, GS, decided that there were meaningful uses of such. I have for

many years thought that GS was potentially a wilder man than he has allowed himself to be, & that he has used Buddhism as a kind of governor on his auto. I got some confirmation for this view from GS himself when I was handed page proofs for *Mountains and Rivers without End,* & noticed that a great section on being high in San Francisco had been left out because it did not "fit" (Gary later told me).

The last poem in the poetry section in *The Grindstone of Rapport,* "The Tjurunga," is an attempt to realize my apprenticework in Kyoto in a present-time construct. I think of the tjurunga as much older than the angel, & as a primary reconstituent link between nature & culture.

Anyway—good morning!   Clayton

*

16 September, 2009

Jung writes that a mandala is a magic circle used as *yantra* (a diagrammatic symbol for a field of energy) to aid (or <u>control</u>) contemplation. "An *inner image* built up through active imagination, at such times when psychic equilibrium is disturbed or when a thought cannot be found and must be sought for, because it is not contained by holy doctrine." *The poem, in other words!*

Jung also writes that "The alleged free and individual formation of the mandala should be taken with a grain of salt, since in all Lamaic mandalas there predominates not only a certain unmistakable style but also a traditional structure." He mentions that mandalas are very old & may even have existed in "paleolithic times." Here he cites certain Rhodesian rock paintings that he does not include photographs or drawings of. Mandalas "signify nothing less than a psychic centre of the personality not to be identified with the ego."

The circular spider web in Kyoto, with spider at center, associated with "powers" such as Coatlicue, Bud Powell, Yorunomado, & César Vallejo (a quaternity, no?) was a kind of homemade mandala. The poem "The Tjurunga" is a mandalesque exercise, a reconstructed labyrinth, not as Lamaic "park" with squared circular forms but a wanderfest or trek into the force field of primary materials. The navigational "recalculatings" represent branchings off, responses to dead ends requiring immediate reorientation. Such are forms, in Fulcanelli's words, of "the *thread of Ariadne* [which] becomes necessary for [the quester] if he is not to wander the winding paths of the task, unable to extricate himself."

James Hillman: "The self depicted in a mandala is a differentiated pattern of polytheistic persons and places. When we make the move, following Jung, from mandala as circle to mandala as integration, the move from an image of roundness to the idea of wholeness, we shall have to bear in mind the shadow of death that is implicated in the mandala… As the Tibetan mandala is a meditative mode that protects the soul from capture by demons, so the Self as an all-embracing wholeness keeps the demonic nature of psychic events from getting through to the soul….

In archaic Western symbolism, the circle is a place of death. We find it in the sepulchral ring or burial barrow later recapitulated in Christian circular churchyards. Both the wheel and the ring (especially as a wreath) may be read as underworld expressions. To be put on the wheel in punishment (as Ixion) is to be put into an archetypal place, tied to the turns of fortune, the turns of the moon and fate, and the endless repetitions of coming eternally back to the same experiences without release… In Celtic myth, the wheel or that which rolls has uncanny, sinister intention. Rings are closed circles and the circle closes on us whether in the marriage band, the crowning laurel, or the wreath on the grave. No way out, which is also how necessity has been defined. The collar ring yoking the neck of a captive slave or prisoner is the oldest meaning of the word *necessity (ananke).* A wheel puts the closed circle into motion, and now we are in a cyclical, compulsive rolling, no end to it."

Contra Hillman: I would propose that part of a poet's responsibilities is to allow "the demonic nature of psychic events" *to get through to the soul.*

30 September, 2009

To be in the tightening gyre of a web
mandalizing, traveling as a center within
a pyramidic complex of sound.

Carnivorous & delicate, the circle is squared,
the womb is cornered, given masculine edge.
Circle & square draw out direction as a bow bends to
 its pull.

Mind as divining rod, vibrant to the Cougnac cave
forever just below,
transmogrified anthem of the psychic center,
eternity tapped,
the square's edges as conscious defilement,
modified womb.

The need of man to four-square himself as if he were circular butter.

In the ash at the base of the soul resides the poem's diadem.

*Every time I raise fork to mouth*
*I evoke the uroboros & see myself entering head-first*
*the intestinal tunnel of the Lascaux bison hovering*
*my dream-flexed erection.*

             Yes, I slayed my father here
but I did not draw the master word from his corpse.
Thus: am I in imagination a knave of an unregenerate Indianapolis?
Or am I alchemically porous,
depending solely upon my own sweat
to inculcate life in the poem?
Here are his tiny bones, *kept as sibyl in the bird cage of my heart.*
For some of the parental burial must be entrusted to the self,
that in its vortex
imagination may conceive a composite figure.

So I sat inside the father skeleton
looking up through the ribs. "Please don't rib me,"
I heard a voice, "I am not Ira C.E. but
Yorunomado, companion 'head hunter,'

the window into night through which
the combat struck within when you disemboweled
confronted by Vallejo."

To imagine from the unground of self,
one's labyrinth (a folded abyss),
the infolded center containing in its pleats
(its pleas, its plaints) the Buchenwald of
"there but for the grace of
*war in the blood forecast & elegized in dream*    go I."

Wholeness is not a master plan nor an *aurora consurgens.*
Wholeness is delivery & burial, a book-ended world
*containing man's misery, woman's compassion,*
another dimension of circle & square.
Wholeness is the full yield of the harrow, including
the seeds, worms, & clods of defenseless baby Clay.

Have we entered the Age of the Holy Synthetic?
The Age in which the genetically modified will become a Godhead
reinforcing unconscious wrath & desperation
to wring out of the creature planet apocalyptic tremors?
Rivers of melt, plains of dryness.
*A new uroboros of deluge & desiccation*
*circling one within the other*
*like a train signal of coral snake coloration.*

    *

                      25 November, 2009

Dying & being: daily pentameter, nightly lasso.
Dial of metamorphosis: the imago within, folded labyrinth.

Elephant or *makara* heads vomiting prong-like wreaths
positioned as part of a mandala's palace doors.

Such heads appear to be planted as fern-like scroll hydrants.
The mandala palace: curling, jagged flames, gold floral & phoenix
    patterns.
A lotus marks the transition (or is it the division?) between
*the divine interior & the ocean of migratory existence encircling it.*

And here are some jewel-bedecked Buddhas meditating within a copper
    alloy lotus mandala.
When closed, we see only a metal lotus on a pillar-like stem—
when opened: eight Buddhas in partial recline
(the tall weapon-like petals function as their recliners).

What is this "nectar of immortality" Buddha Amitāya is said to hold?
*Pure inspiration?* But this lotus mandala is shaped by & loaded with
    *tradition.*

At root, there is emptiness, prior to & beyond being:
nebula forests, star caves illuminated with opium-like cliffs
dustifying in eternal night, my art as my afterlife.

What does it mean *to ride a lion?* To mentally saddle feline voracity?
To be driven through circular causation by one's instinctive will?
Or is this *a lion of stone?* Death roaring under one's ass as one flits,
hungry glowworm, through the flames of "pristine awareness"?

Who is an emanation of who—or what?
Female as male emanation has it all backwards in Buddhism as well as
    Blake.

Who doesn't have a boar head attached to his own?

Who doesn't yearn for animal stasis, immeasurable & eternal?

What man doesn't dream of a syncopated wholeness, his "other" in his
arms & rotating
    on his diamond trident?

The ocean of migratory existence is presented as the charnel grounds circle surrounding the palaces in which the Buddha emanations, multi-legged, multi-armed, multi-headed, wearing necklaces of freshly-severed heads, supplied with arrows, bows, skull cups, staffs, curved knives, & wearing buffalo masks, ride lions, dance & fuck.

I see Fred Astaire with his dakini Ginger Rogers when I look at these multi-legged & -armed dervishes in copulational sashay. Astaire decked out in muted plaid suit, a soft button-down shirt, pale woven tie, silk pocket hankie, bright horizontally-striped hose & white bucks! Mickey Mouse merged with Bach in grasshopper lightness, studied friviolity, great concentration, constantly in doubt & anger over his work. A bejeweled shadow Buddha with pixy-nimble tread.

Where am I in all of this? Undoubtedly in the charnel circle, naked, with an eye to the palace. What happens if I climb up, out, & *in*?

Is the initiated body the organless one sought by Artaud? Note his dancing "diamond body" at the end of *To Have Done with the Judgment of God*:

> When you have given him a body without organs
> then you will have delivered him from all his automatisms and
>     restored him to his true liberty.

> Then you will teach him again to dance inside out
> as in the delirium of dance halls
> and that inside out will be his true side out.

Blake evokes these palace-enshrined yab-yums on the 28th Plate of his *Jerusalem* where Albion & Vala are portrayed in sexual union in a floating lotus flower. A headless caterpillar is seen emerging from their leafy tryst, as if the phallus is skedaddling so to move the lovers from three-fold pleasure to four-fold bliss.

Is Saint Anthony up to his temptations? Saint as dead center. Temptations as the frolicking ghastliness (from Hieronymus Bosch's point of view) inherent in the saint's resistance.

Only those mandalas with charnel circles strike me as essentially human. These outer circles are a marvelous carnival of corpse dumping grounds, dreamscape, hell, religious practice, sensual pleasure, & sheer imaginative weirdness. Bosch seems to have studied charnel circles. Floating bones, severed heads. In the top of a tree a white guardian called "Elephant Face". Stake-impaled hanging bodies. Liberated souls as well as hungry ghosts. A cloud called "Making Sounds". Leopards & long-necked birds eating corpses. Deities & guardians meditating on cushions, outstretched bodies, animals, *makaras.* Dakinis with serpent tails. Dancing boar-headed men. A bull-headed snake. Floating torso chunks. At the top of another tree a red guardian called "Crocodile Face". Demons flogging naked recumbents. Old one-armed women in vermilion gowns stretched out on couches. Pitch-black skies, full red moons. At the foot of a *bataki* tree a guardian called "Possessing a Rosary of Human Heads"; he is naked, blue, clutches a sword & skull cup & rides a zombie. Naked lovers enjoying tea. Many stupas. A red-headed man releasing an arrow as he himself shoots out of a tree…

I wonder to what extent the palaces packed with dancing deities & guardians surrounded by outlying charnel ground rings mirror life in medieval Tibetan society where, according to Michael Parenti's *Friendly Feudalism: The Tibet Myth,* the Dalai Lama's 1000 room 14 story Potala Palace was surrounded by a fiefdom system of slavery, unpaid labor, crushing taxes, children conscripted for life-long servitude as domestics, dance performers & soldiers, as well as eye-gougings, hamstringings & amputation as forms of criminal punishment. In short, a theocracy that equated rebellious thought & action with satanic influence, codified by teachings about the karmic residue of virtue & vice accumulated from past lives, all of which were presented as part of God's will.

*A Grotesque Mandala*

He holds her by both buttocks
eases her onto his erection
looks into her perfectly beautiful face
fantasying that the rear of her skull is a marsh of worms.
For centuries they have swayed
in an open circular casket
set within a square casket,
the circular one being of wood, the square of metal,
the interaction of wood & metal
providing their orgone fuel.
               And there is more:
the anaconda of the west has been given an enema,
it coils, flexing as if in birth throes, over their heads.
This enema is the enemy of the diamond & the womb
symbolized by square & round caskets:
*brown rain* is what it says
*brown desdain* of the ancient manticore trumpeting
tornado-wise over all heads...


No liberation from the anus of the seraphim.
All your ideals, all your liquid self-regard
are as a bed of tacks to
               these swayers
convulsant & lateral
king & queen pins,
angel shadows in the forest of our
masculinist host.

# WOODEN SPOON

Scrubbing out the grit in the spoon cracks before stirring
just-starting-to-boil wild rice.

Old, fifteen years in spoon life, maybe a hundred in ours,
without paint, décor, or machine polish, sweetly rough to my hand.

Essence of that which enables.
Evocation of prehensile pride.

Dear sister particle:
to grasp you as 73 years ago I sought my mother's breast.

Stirring as part of our cosmological rotation.

Shoulderless spoon: extra-terrestrial on a stick.

# DAY OF THE DEAD, 2009

Wood box storefront. Eight celebrating skeletons.
No room to really kick up their bony heels, so they jostle—
one fellow plucks a 10 string armadillo-shell harp.
Six tortillas forever ready to be served on the skull rack
   slant through humanity
while our drones hit Afghanistan & thousands of Americans troop
   in and out.
               Do the dead today
just press against the sigils in our dreams,
not even making smudges on the glass we awake to?
Relative to the power of the stars,
are we no more than gas nebulae robed in translucent leather?


              One of my box skeletons wears
  a Karzai cap,   another tilts a vase to his skull's
painted teeth.
            Courageous Nancy Spero sambas through
    brandishing a dildo of fire.

# HOVERING LARA GLENUM *

Lara Glenum is crawling toward a crocodile crawling toward her.
Osmotic exchange of DNA Dodgem.
Marvelous head-fire as Nubian centuries exchange photons.
Soon the Glenum head will penetrate the croc muzzle.
Is Glenum now more alive, more griffin than grail maid?
To be green & dentilated in tongue & casing.
*Maximum Gaga* is the grave of the literal,
of the monotale, death of descriptive cheesyness,
for the mind is now in croc goddess crawl formation
beseeching *mantle* to be *mortar, mother* to burp *Merlin,*
   or *aardvark* or *moraymoon.*
The head of Orpheus now aslit & porous to a fin-handed leech queen
percolating his brain coral with servings of menstrual mud.
Inanna as a dragonfly emblazoned on the dial of the human:
to infiltrate its astral sewers with insectile halos,
to inhabit all its Darwin nesting dolls,
to hear *metaphor* as imaginal transfer to the Siamese croc
pustulating "my cunt a violent surge-hammer
         in the mouth of the Redeemer."

# FOR MY NIECE LIANA *

Music **apologizes**
for what we are,   have been,
will do. Is this why
E.M. Cioran loves, of the arts, only music?
Tone is outside of articulation (argument),
tone as modulated silence, instantly
whole,   a Babel bolt
—for what we have done to love?

Waiting to hear you sing tonight I associate back:
*fire place,*   vulva to which a fagot is touched—
Ignition is woman.   Sparks swirling campfire chat—music?
55,000 year old Divje Babe cave bear femur
pierced by spaced holes—the earliest known flute…

The oldest myth may be the story of the creatures who dove into the
     deep
to bring up the stuff of which the earth was made.
What was heard when this duck or dung beetle surfaced,
     mud in its mouth?
Aurora's gracile grackle?

          At her Boston University recital,
          20 March 2009

# FOR KEN MIKOLOWSKI   *

Is here heir to our being all is can?
Or are all, is, shells under which no pea?

If nothing is under all is not all nothing as is?
And if all has no pea might it not be a chasm of vanished we?

Night is evening's clouded brine in which kobold shadows loom.
Night is a still in which our mother's heart, a sun hammer,
keens for her straying brood.

Would childhood still have flavor were we to bite its consoling blank?
Would we then say: in the silage of our vanishing
there are pearls mixed in with perils?

Or would we say: no wave ever tastes this swell.
That is, all, like nothing, are the dearth which is
our wealth & moil?

Tarantula amble of my tips, trestle of their sympathetic tree.

Ghost simulacra in knotted, furrowed trunks:
the "dog" in "Erdogan," in "slovenly" the "love"
as if all libido is accessed from the read.

Vertiginous trail, more shadow trial than sand.
Even clouds feed on God's eyelash atmos fairs!

Death knell birth ring, gong gone
thirst ripple, nipple emitting dust.

The weeks as clapper prattle. The years as whispering bells.

# FOR DON MEE CHOI  *

You belong to none except the gong.
*On* to *on* its copper undulations translate into meat—
the cheek of liberty, Ensoresque crowds.
Your self behind yourself concealed,
what Hadic invisibility is being revealed?
Is your forehead apotropaic from wandering in your face?
Or did you drop the soul hammer seconds before
    the bong?

Cambodia with four million of our land mines.
Bankers glinting crystal angles.
You're in Seattle. I'm outside Detroit.
We're both facing the light show in Club Rapture.
The planet is an ongoing Rave. Afghan bands on LSD
while American drones chowder their family bunks

1962: I am bargaining with a Korean whore in discarded
GI fatigues by
the Seoul SAC Compound Gate.
The dispossessed & the poet
before the closed Western Gate:
we lack the power to realize what we see to be real.

Its all absurd &
eerily mantic: the fabricator of our uterine
scaffolding keeps shadowing our present shade.

You belong to a longing to birth rapids & mares,
to a rampart on which a *hagazussa* is oiling her broom.
You look down a cerebral tunnel rotating with escapes:
                        all harrowing enough
to keep you focused on a phantomatic art.

Were you to insert a serpent, might "the lambent
homage of his arrowy tongue" turn you into a pythoness
capable of resetting a cosmogonic dial?

Ransacked by our finite infinity,
we hover the anima gore stored in testicular vats.

# A HALF HOUR WITH BASQUIAT   *

Skull trash staring through wall splash.
Face skillet with sunny-side-up red eyeballs.
Black heel sprouting splayed white fingers.
We have no Hades,    only fetus graffiti!

Halo in a state of wire-barbed garble.
Words a pickup-sticks melee,    a Styx of bloated
   Charon heads,   out of "syncopation" staggers
     *sin  cop  nation,*  the hero din of heroin wind.
"O war within my members!"
Pit bull in a wedding dress trailing bloodied brail.

Is Basquiat's angel aware of its incarnation in ashes,
its wholeness in spit-swiped absence?
Its arrows, spirals, half-effaced, misspelled words?
Its word-antlered
     ant hives of
   mutant lewd
      imprecations?

Ours, the Aeon of the Child, "Crowned & Conquering."

The only sin is self-restriction. Detritus as the nullity soul of vision.

Skull as a dream meal, including knives, forks & bone cake chewings.

[Gagosian Gallery, NYC, 3 April 2013]

# FOR JOYELLE MCSWEENEY  *

Joyelle McSweeney writes that she wants to unlock her phone.

At 80, I want to unlock my absence, enter afterlife here.
To use every bit of my it essence.
To not merely pocket with my 80 year 8 ball the ghosts of my own
   asshole.

My commas, like curling up armadillos, are becoming periods,
gargoyle monocles, wizened atavisms staring down.

When death ceases to be conceptual, precision writhes as it meets time.

I now lie in duplex strata, less stalk than tassel dance.

The feeling of being a nail
vertically
afloat
over the gravity of hole
pullulation.

# FOR RODIN

Psyche is
unfinished
realized
marble

—a dream grasped in
a subjectile
roving marine depth,
antiphonal.

Foaled stone,
granitic gramophone,
siren-swarmed...

the mind of which
I ride.

# COMPOST OF THE MOMENT

During dinner, at times, I sink into
a Wales of unknown lingo,
a post-American or
pre-Biblical furrow. I wonder if
this plinth will crack
where only self is central.
Harold Bloom adores the Whitmanian "myself,"
sublime ego pump, but when we range
Duncan, Olson & Ginsberg, Rothenberg, Eshleman & Kelly become
    wilderness to
Yale intelligence.   So,
I am sitting here in my tank,
the waters of the world & my own are,
for a while, even! Whew, for once, but
instantly a bomb goes off in Mogadishu
I am vexed it has something to do with my taxes
so    I am a taxi driver in Kinshasa,
"nice afternoon for rape" Now I'm a snakehead
feeding Chinese refugees into Chinatown,
O'Hara's "Grace to be born…" is nigh
sipping the last of the Punto Final
after a delicious rack of lamb with Caryl.
Marinated in the brains of the mask:
compost of the moment.
At the N.O. Brown Drive-in Theater tonight:
screened fleas, fleeting amphimixian arrows.

# SELF AS SELVA   *

It is a fine autumn Sunday & my tourniquet has just turned on.

Robert A.F. Thurman: "According to the Buddha, the reality of all things is ultimate selflessness. And this experience of turning around in the depth of the self from self-delusion and self-obsession to freedom and concern for others is the fountain of Buddhistic energy. Possessing an independent self at the core of one's being is a delusion. Selflessness is a description of the experienceable condition of the living self, which obviously does exist, and obviously is not a static, independent, isolated, or alienated entity. Seeing through the false sense of rigid self releases a person from the imprisoning sense of alienation from the universe. The Buddha devised a host of methods and techniques to assist people to realize their own selflessness, freedom, and compassion."

Or as Wallace Stevens put it: "losing in self / The sense of self…"

H.P. Lovecraft: "To know that one is no longer a definite being distinguished from other beings—that one no longer has a self—that is the nameless summit of agony and dread."

William Blake: "The Spectre… is the Great Selfhood
Satan: Worshipd as God by the Mighty Ones of the Earth
Having a White Dot calld a Center from which branches out
A Circle in continual gyrations. this became a Heart
From which sprang numerous branches varying their motions
Producing many heads three or seven or ten, & hands & feet
Innumerable at will of the unfortunate contemplator
Who becomes his food such is the way of the Devouring Power"

Once we have cast off the self's hood, are we left with pure self?

"A dynamic unstable agglomerate of *skandas* that in itself posses no inherent substantiality or enduring quality and that continues in constant flux until final dissolution at death"

Ah, the selzer of self, the carbonated, carboniferous antiquity of the ever-
evaporating self!

Sylph, or elf, as if figments of self,
gaseous particles that make up that "White Dot calld a Center,"
past lives, or dream incursions, the forge of nightmare,
one's chest as anvil on which a Muse-muzzled succubus crouches
pounding energy deposits into the helpless dreamer?
No, the dreamer is self's help-mate, receiving, like 9 inch spikes,
these elf & sylph deposits, the souls of eaten animals,
one's own dead, those who sip at the *ofrenda* feasts;
below conscious personality: a trillion butterflies pulsate,
a World Tree of sorts, drawing up into their broad wings
the breath of one's dead.
                                        Is it this conglomerate
presence / non-presence of the dead that complexes the Self?

As I walk down the street, on different planes, in different directions,
galleys are stroking through the liquid self that makes up my being,
nebulous continuum open to incursion from the moment of conception.
Who or what has assigned specific rowers to these galleys?
Some wear wolf masks, some are headless, some I'd swear are
conscious & subconscious spliced organisms—
hybrid animal souls swirl up in dream,
curl here, in these necro-nectar vials, these words...

        *

Inspiration: shadow of the Samuel Greenberg falcon with Hart Crane's
nape in its talons...

Or Vallejo drawing a bull's eye on my gut...

What I want is a topocosmic center,
the imaginal order of a particular place,

an ever-evolving god to withstand the merging of different cultures,
    different myths…

We no longer sacrifice bulls to Zeus, but a slanting Akashic microphone
picks up Font-de-Gaume convexities,
there are bison here as intangible as the concavities of Iraq.

The quest is always to abandon one's starting blocks,
set fire to the track under one's soles,
flip away the winner cord, eliminate the track & set forth
with all other runners into the suburbs or wilds,
searching for the birdserpent in one's heart…

Northrop Frye: "Blake saw that as long as man lives within a hierarchical
myth without really knowing it, his whole behavior will be conditioned
beyond the point of resistance: a rebellion against one hierarchy will merely
set up a second one."

Frye again: "From the point of view of the creative mind, consciousness is
a partial and premature unification of mental powers, and what is needed
for creation is a new bicameral mind in which something else supplements
consciousness."

Might that "something else" be identified as "a midden of the instant?"

Identity in the indefinite.
Antiphonal slingshots "mixing" day & night minds.
Honeysuckle sweet worm cast perfume interlacing arctic crystalline
    breeze.
Self-regulatory anarchy.

Not to eliminate self (as in Nirvana) but to become an infanite in the infi-
nite, infantrailed, permeated with the absence to come; welfaring the cen-
ter, farewelling the periphery. Minotaur wedlock. Lightning-bolt love.

The gods have animal minds. The totem pole salmon-raven-beaver-bear "folk": a DNA double helix evocation.

Self as selva, a liana matrix of twin-twisted lingo.

# THE EYE MAZES OF UNICA ZÜRN *

The impossible is as alive as a millipede in furl with its scurry.
A Morpho on morphine a morphology of musical mayhem.
Lines fluttering a vast delicate skirt seamed with snakes,
ocellated lines, lines skittering into fleshy, insectile trains.

Are there not eyes in all things, things tolling in all eyes?
Do the eyes of a stone close facing the beheading of Giordano Bruno
or do they moisten so as to harbor petroglands of blood?
Eyes & fish lips in heads inside a head: galaxies of eyes.

Unica as a dragonfly on stilts giant-stepping through Kokodera.

*

"Who," Unica asks, "will choose me?
In the outback of the face will all the eyes burst,
blistering me with pupil chiggers?

Or is that just you Michaux?
Are you the rabbit-fairy-flea intent upon my catastatic excavation?

As long as I have rubberneck eyes I can lock onto my nipples,
visit the oysters in my breasts.

There is this black ace of a face
nibbled at by faceted, eye-mazed, extra-terrestrial questers."

*

I am studying a double page from Unica Zürn's unpublished illustrated
manuscript *Orakel und Spektakle,* dated in one spot "Paris, April, 1960."
This is her Garden of Ediacara, millions of years before Eden, Unica's
"Dream Time." Multicellular organisms whose mouths are simple open-

ings surrounded by tentacles, leafy "fingers," plumose fringes & tangled masses as if torn from a lion's mane. A stinging forest of near-creatures turning into arthopods that metamorphize upon recognition.

Fraying armored centipedal ferns drifting across a busy many-eyed, petal-skinned human head.

A giant octopus "involved" with the bisected rippling body of a wraith who has an eye-lined disintegrating arm.

Unica has penned in some German phrases which crawl these algae-like proliferations, tagging them into our time.

\*

I watch Unica pupilize, puppetize, then flea bait her range.
I note the rotary palimpsest of all the men inhabiting her facial levers, motordrome cylinders on whose vertical walls eyes cycle defying gravity. Moon of cratered nests in which eye spiders drink her strength.

# IMAGES OUT OF IRAN, JUNE 2009

June 16. Along Valiasr Street, From Enghaleb to Freedom Square,
18 km.
        I see Ophelia crawling The Milky Way.


Clash of my dread, bewilderment, & hope for these people.
On the computer screen they look like a confetti river,
a flower-clustered slow pour, green salamanders rippling.


A single organism, in the spirit that a termite mound is one,
Mousavi their Queen:
        his face: a veronica on a follower's cloth mask.


The crowds pour on, as if through sieves of knowing
percolating their understandable cries for recount, for release:
        to scrape the rusted god crust from their bread


Were the subconscious of everyone alive to be wrung,
might the truth press forth?
                Hold on:
the subconscious is without jurisprudence,
its autos do not crash, they slice through one another
tumbling into the cenotes of history where
the slain for no reason
the slain unknowns & those not slain
(but unaccounted for) fail to age....


Veiled housewives who might feel in this jostle-winding
a being-at-large who would not possess them...


The shade of Whitman, commenting as if from his pantheon:
"I see Teheran... This face is a life-boat.
This is the face commanding and bearded, it asks no odds of the rest.
This face is flavor'd fruit, ready for eating.
This face of a healthy honest boy is the programme of all good."

The naivete of this crowd, this thronging, this crusade,
this snail blessing of mortals pressing toward a mystical,
democratic sun they believe will receive them,
will not obliterate their yearning for happiness.

Were I there, I'd be with them,
as lost, as self-sure, of what lies in wait?
Around the corner of a decree?
In the ballot drop under a fanged gate?

For Joe Phillips

# WHILE DRINKING COFFEE AT ZINGERMAN'S *

Night of the Congo, wreath
of raped women, horrors beyond
augury,   here in Ypsilanti
it's a crumbly basement wall surface, out there
instant communication of fate
massive poisoned umbrella, under which—stop here,
Peter Rabbit,    Eden is enfolded smoke, & the fox has entered
your sperm,    "Rebecca Kamate"
repeatedly raped after being forced to lie on top of
her chopped-up Congo husband's body parts.
I envision her & her raped daughters then asking the Buddha:
is this what you mean by "suffering?"
Dilemma of this post hole in the mind,
dilemma of the absolute in any guise, driving prick
or camauro. Can't allow religion or
any "spiritual practice" outside of poetry to direct.
At 74, I'm my own weathervane,
in robe of insomnia, & the sweet graze of
near sleep,   Caryl's magically soft
underarm, a light rub, what we call "a tickle,"
watching Keith Olbermann go after the Blue Dogs,
more commercials than news in 45 minutes,
fuck it, go to sleep, or drift awake…


Kevin Davies' "Lateral Argument" is *Howl* brayed fine,
   compassion minced with fury,
rage jump-cut with loopy minutiae, perceptively random,
word texture like a cross-wired crowd…


This great June 16th Teheran crawl of jostle-winding being,
this cosmic caterpillar,   like Sibelius's 7th   loaded
with finality,   V-fingered hands waggling,   overflown by
the angel Sorush in bright-green helmet, beaked seabird wings—
where was this "we" in Gore's dazed 2000 election face?

Drain of religion armed with the bomb of immortality.
Churches the size of small planets on military bases.
Religion is the locked-down imagination of eternal war.

Think of this life as your base, not as your whole subject.
Be grateful for asymmetrical lettuce, the design of a bay.
See through hate: it is redolent with rejectitious dread.
Robin Blaser near his end wrote: "Language is love."
Not at Sobibor. Or even in smashed abortion clinic signs.
Experience & language mingle on a psychic plane penetrable by poetry.
And once poetry gets "in between,"
one almost needs the density of "Lachrymae Christi"
to realize the contravention.

# STITT HORNS IN  *

Rounding the gym track listening to WEMU.
Suddenly Sonny Stitt entangles "Koko" with my mental vines.

"Cherokee" lyrics, schlock "Indian romance,"
pulled inside out by "Koko," "Cherokee's" vital ghost.

Euphotic zone where there's stride foam I can drink.
Is it mitotic?  Is it mine?

To incurvate
our nature, animals volley through.
Megaceroses, aurochses, ripe as fountains.
From whence this meta-image-music?
Does psyche rise from the void?
Or is the unground inhabited by Pan, satyrs, dog-headed baboons?

In each animal the ark recapitulated!
*Imago dei,* the animal face of our finite nature.
A megaceros-mounted goddess. Birth of the altar beast.
Aura in which my skeleton is dancing, a Minotaur in
    a gaseous time fugue.
Palimpsestic pad of a polar bear's paw.
Read it as a god palm. See through division.

James Hillman: "Each polar bear presents the eternal return of the polar
    bear spirit
as a guardian, a spiritus rector, from which, according to Ivar Paulson,
    speaking of
circumpolar arctic peoples, the very idea of God arises."

Now Stitt pours on more "Koko" anti-freeze:
as if out of Goya, a black sorcerer goat
stares at me
out of a white goat ocean.

Word spars churn a depth fantasia.
The pressure always: to penetrate my fate.

And what is fate? Our red maple breaking into a massacre of leaves?
A vulture alighting behind a bunched-up starveling?

Am I coming to terms with the strata of vitriol I've mined?

Here to gauge the depth of my plumb line—
how open my fontanel was to the toxicities of my times.

I once passed through a smoking gate, turned back & glimpsed
(caught in a photo, 1969)   Caryl, with my "Regeneration" in her arms.

And realization?  Right here, in the Orphic head
I've bowled into the bones of experience.

# THE STAIN

Where I sleep, on the sheet
I lie & twist on, there is a stain this morning, as if last night
certain daemons, unhappy to be flesh-curbed,
slipped downward, gravity driven.

Animal matrix, are you thinning? Legacy of
infant perturbation, are you amassing atavistic legions?
Or am I fooled by this jester exit, this ageglass drip?

Naked to night's minutiae as well as to the great night
with its vortex abyss in the Milky Way—
to what degree am I connected to the matriarchal
infinity of plant & star? To sacrificial flesh or
Taino *canoa* afloat on swells my mind can barely tap?

This morning, staring at my stain, I accept
the carnal exile of this hybrid absence:
*I was there, I dreamed of layered*
*Minotaurs grafted to wounded messengers,*
*a self-engaged passion at the hub of the labyrinth…*

It is from this dripstone
my imaginal omphalos was formed.

"The rite at the hunting site, given to the souls of the animal killed, was thus basic, in the sense that it was addressed to its soul-essence and the general fertility of the species."

This is Weston La Barre in *The Ghost Dance,* 1972.   I keep driving by these run-over squirrels, & the distance between the rite La Barre cites *and*
our feel for dead animals today,
especially the ones we kill
—they are glassy blood flesh black hair,
   organs mashed, stripes of animal, no animal,
      just mash, driven over again & again—

Those sleeping along the sides of roads throughout America,
the sleeping squirrels, the sleeping chipmunks, the fat crushed wood-
   chucks.

My own demise is singular. These are Whitmanian multitudes.

The white baby rabbit taking a nap, the beagle showing off its splayed
   groin,
   all the animals
now waiting for the Rapture when we will cease to run them over.

We have lost the great omentum, the nutrient sac of compassion,-
   renewal,
   guilt for having killed.

I'm enraged by something deeper than I can grasp—

*That prayer for renewal has been turned into disregard*

   SO WHAT
         Get to the cleaners on time.

# NORTH TOWER EXPLODING  *

10:28 AM:
top of the Tower: the antenna spire
begins to descend before any movement occurs in the exterior walls
(suggesting the Tower's collapse begins with the destruction of
what supports the antenna: the building's fireproof core columns)

How could the debris crush 96 steel & concrete floors
*while* surging earthward at the speed of gravity?
Each floor shattered *before* the debris above it made contact
i.e., the debris never *collided* with any floors.

Most of the jet fuel was gone in the initial fire ball.
Black smoke = oxygen starved fires suffocating.
Jet fuel cannot melt steel or iron—
molten steel needs 2750°F to melt.

1,434 people murdered.

Over a hundred fell or jumped to their obliteration.

The first departure occurred 4 minutes after the first plane hit, from the
149th window of the 93rd floor on the north face of the building. The
"cascade" began 7 minutes later, with 13 falls in 2 minutes.

People hugging or holding hands as they fell together.

Did Eddie Torres jump?

Terminal velocity 120 MPH; up to 200 MPH if the person fell with the
body straight.

Karen Juday identified by her husband in a photograph wearing the
familiar bandana she always put on at work, standing in a window frame,
holding on, flames behind her.

Edna Citron seen waving out from a deep gash in the North Tower,
smoke & flames behind her.

"I think most of the 'jumpers' actually lost their grip while gasping for
air and were eventually burned out of the building by all the searing
smoke, burning up their hands, burning up their backs."

"It was raining bodies. They were jumping now, one, two, three, four,
smashing like eggs on the ground."

Man in a white waiter's jacket, black pants, black high-tops,
photographed by Richard Drew, frozen in a head-first dive, came to be
known as The Falling Man.

Norberto Hernandez?

Jonathan Briley?

"Little people falling like fairies."

"Some tried parachuting until the force generated by the fall ripped the
drapes, the tablecloth, the desperately-gathered fabric, from their hands."

"They were like big ketchup stains with clothing on top."

*

21,300 windows
300,000 square feet of glass
100,000 tons of structured steel
2,500,000,000 square feet of gypsum
3 acres of marble
212,000 cubic feet of concrete *become*

horror dumps of pulverized debris,
molten metal flowing down into the rubble piles,

large salmon-yellow pools of molten metal in the post-collapse base-
    ment—
the end products of a radio-computer-initiated firing from Building 7
    using super-thermite matches?

Unspent aluminothermic explosives & matching residues
    were found in the Tower's dust

        Karen Juday's jawbone

along with Adolf Rumsfeld's turned-off cell phone.

# THE OCCUPIED LIFE

East Timor is "stable." This must mean that the Indonesian Army,
supplied by USA, is on a rampage.
The beheaded are calm. The sky is fluttering a Pinochet kite
whose stabilizing tail is the knotted entrails of thousands.
Dressed up as a caterpillar, I am contemplating Tenochtitlan.
My butterfly belongs to the state, so I remain larval,
a presence you may notice to
the left of the broccoli.
                                    The German painter Horst Haack writes:
"Very strange. Your September 11 theory is shared now by even the most
popular magazines like 'Stern' and "Spiegel' and nobody seems to care or
bother. Everyone expects the worst from Washington. If a paper reported
that Bush Jr. as a new hobby was shooting Arab-terrorist prisoners on his
ranch Sunday afternoon, readers would believe it—show the President
holding a gun and everyone would take that for proof."


Never has personal life here been at
a greater discrepancy with
the state of the union. Never has the use of God,
in my lifetime, been more bizarre,
has Presidential glossolalia (2005) needed
so much translation, or simple inversion of meaning.
Never, Poet Laureate Glück, was your post more ridiculous.
Never was Blake's praise of Los
—"He kept the divine vision in a time of trouble"—
more sage.


And what might "divine vision" mean today?
"The imagination spans beyond despair…"
not God but integrity to the precipice of the instant,
adherence to the otter as well as to
the subconscious ball court of the dead.

So I donned my wasp-nest headdress & apologized to Gaza—
outside my workroom window, life at large still looks swell.
What hypnogogic power lurks in that "swell."
Turn on the computer, the pain chart starts to zig-zag,
like a rip in Kafka's kidney, it swells into plump, pulpy wounds.
And yet—the ivy on neighbor Emily's brick has never been greener.
This is the Bush junta's steepest hope:
that neighborhood serenity will wall off the sea of blood
    pooling in our awareness.

27 May 2005

# MIND TOMBS

JFK must have been assassinated by the powers he was going up against. Ditto Bobby.

If Obama had gone after Bush & Cheney, as well as others responsible for the dustification of the three WTC towers & the bogus WMD claims that "justified" our invasion of Iraq, would he be alive today?

For the kind of people in back of Kennedy's death, as well as ML King's, 3000 dead in Manhattan is a tiny chip in a war promo.

Mind tombs: delvings & speculations one believes are true but for which there is no open investigation, indictment—or closure.

How explain the ongoing failure to disclose & to root out the shadow government that is may be responsible for all these deaths?

I gave a dollar in change to a guy at an off ramp today. He had a sign: SINGLE FATHER CHILDREN NEED FOOD. How fucked up I felt scratching in the coin pot for what I could grab for him before the light changed.

Between that man & the children rummaging for computer parts in world electronic dumps, there is immense &     *no distance.*

Dreams shuffle these mind tombs, then deal them out to the assassinated assembly in hands only comprehensible to them.

To then look outside & in the moonlight see an injured scorpion dragging herself through the grass loaded with 900,000 Iraqi widows.

# A MORNING WRITHING WITH REVELATION *

[Bacon & Giacometti at Gagosian]

Being here as an enraptured trap, an entrapture.

In John Edward's shadow there is dark matter digesting his simian
borders.

Giacometti's gropentangled maya maze. Erase nothing.
(How can Nothing be erased?)

Bacon mayhem make-up: rouged New Guinea eyes by skillet heat
widened.

Diego breasted in rubble: hoof-legged arms, a lap of Mars.

Hacked-into eaten-out Bacon head, riverine blood-lined hair

Car crashes babooning in Henrietta Moraes' tusk-thrusty laughter.

Mohawked George Dyer, a semen-mouthed turbine in a slather of bulbs
& rags.

Milking a man out of an udder fist: fornicate, whistling fission gist.

        This is the morgue of a mandala.
My efforts are to unleash the spirits of words,
to amble with & intoxicate their agencies
so that the morgue empties by the second
as new lines pour through.

And what exactly are these black discs set into some of these Bacon
portraits?
The immobile, uncanny, unlightable lakes in humankind?

James Hillman: "This would be the ultimate task of soul-making and its beauty: the incorporation of destruction into the flesh and skin, embalmed in life, in the visible transfigured by the invisibility of Hades' kingdom, anointing the psyche by the killing experience of its personal mortality."

Or are these discs Bacon's versions of black holes?
Indicating that we are in the final stages of our species' history?

That like certain stars, we can no longer produce "expansive force"?

That nothingness is now pregnant with the isolational reality of our being?

29 November 2008

# OIL SPILL

Oil-stained white caps tossing,
sluggish mire, scarlet swirling luster.

Cobalt oil worms: welts lolling.

Bottlenose dolphins nosing up under oil:
nebulae of white, limpid gas.

Clots & blackened larvae, torque of water drape.

Crepe-stiff blue-black islands.
One, foot-shaped,
streamed by mucous-blue sheens.

Blobs of offal pebbles, roan static sea.

Mississippi marsh framed by maroon-black slick.
The death of Rothko.

Split crimson snake, butchered
dolphin loaf,
beauty-lewd eco-horror.

Oil slick containing in its lavender gloss
a black tree-like configuration:
Olson's 1968 eaten-out World Tree?   Update:
Tree rotted through,   its flattened
saurian      ghost                  spreading.

31 May 2010

# EARTHQUAKE

Swarming flies.  Charnel house bubbling.
Vigilantes. Roadblock barriers.

Lightning-struck Vodun center-post, loas milling.
Supply planes over the corpse of Port-au-Prince, Léogâne.

"A *Shabbat* from hell, the acrid smell of bodies rotting…"
No more polar bears.
Oh Haiti—solely killer whales.

    *

Oh Haiti, loas milling the migratory ocean of striving.

Children with severe fractures affixed solely with cardboard.

World as a mandala with Doc & Baby Doc demons.

The corpse of Port-au-Prince, Léogâne.
Hunger rape & looting across the nation's,
quake-split teeming soul.

    *

Humans spiked on the poles of a bloated world mandala.
"It is just like the stories we were told of the Holocaust"
Throughout the destruction: bodies
in numbers no one can begin to grasp.

Max Beauvoir, Vodun priest, protests
the lack of dignity in mass burials.

Oh Haiti, brain-cruising demons
heard singing throughout the night.

\*

Oh Haiti
humans adrift in the surging migratory ocean of striving.

No more polar bears.
Doc & Baby Doc demons circulating
this nation's quake-split soul.

World as a bubbling charnel grounds.

The corpse of Port-au-Prince, Léogâne

Loas circle as planes with supplies.

Hunger rape & looting.

      20 January, 2010

# CHROMATIC LESIONS

Amphigoric love of language & its vinous analogues.

To live one's *not* in all its flamboyant stagnation.

Nothing is *not*   revealed

Wind swept impermanence of this endless winch.

                    Yet this autumn is beautiful, & beautiful
even loss underscored by sound sleep.

I have sealed my own destructiveness, cauterized its principle feelers.

And now recall my first sense of dread:
I was 7, on the living room sofa with my parents
at my grandparents' home in Elkhart
listening to grandpa read a letter from their ex-Russian lodger
writing the Eshleman family about the horrors of the siege of Leningrad.

Everything is (and has never been) a milling, amorphous terribilita
searching for a craving out of which to be born.

I have learned to see
   in the faces of the dead
a jug of rose-white chickadee explosion.

# BERDACHE

Under my childhood bed, using the dark to become. Arranging soldiers, head to head, the dark dear, & me in my little ark, snuggled next to Sparky or Ginger, my Irish terrier familiars. To nest, as a child to cease being a child, to draw on the floor, finger wandering insignias of no. To feel the ark edge, the limit of my caul. To be, just a bit.

In my closet doorway to sit, & turn on my 8 mm projector, watching cartoons. Then to draw my own, Crummy and Dummy, little crows in robes. Based on the Katzenjammer Kids, crows acting up, inklings of moving as another, not having a self but wanting a myself, "anywhere out of this world."

Sparky & then Ginger lived in the back of our garage in an enclosure my father constructed with a little door to an outside pen. Over the enclosure was a narrow loft reached by a ladder, for tools & occasionally for me, barefoot in one of my mother's dresses. The dress allowed me to twist about, I thought, like a dog & pretend to have pups. Sparky once had eight.

Tell how I returned to her womb. Tell how I wrapped in her organs, how I struggled there not to be born, but to move from under-bed-space to closet-doorway-space to loft-over-Sparky-enclosure where no one could hear me yelling my first made up curse: "Goddamn black widows!" "Goddamn black widows!" very loud.

# THE GOOD MOTHER

Be rent so as to let
the brownies in, the whistling, capering trickster folk,
tiny engines of kelson ramifications…

Mano a mano of the nascent self
evoking mandala densities, unlived charnel blockages,
lemur snickerings, as if one had just been kicked out of
one's pack, stranded
in the buckeye out of which
Bobby Hook pulled me down & I yelled for my mother

blew through our front door whirl-
encircling Bobby & me with "Darling
the earth did not invite you,
the earth is indifferent to your charm,
the earth is here as a mantle, wear it & be warned."

And with that she was gone
leaving me in my dirty skirt & with the neighborhood bully's
three eyes punched out.

# VELMAR'S LEMON

August 1952, Indianapolis, terrible heat. Shortridge High School daily
football practice, three hours in the morning, three in the afternoon.
Full equipment. Our coach was George Gale, in tee-shirt, unpadded
silver pants, with his huge calves. He also wore anklets with snazzy low-
cut cleated shoes. Someone said he had briefly been a professional field-
goal kicker. I'd get up at 7 A.M., breakfast & bicycle to the practice field.
By 9 we were in our dank full uniform. To then pound ourselves for
three hours. I'd bicycle home for lunch. Mother made me creamed beef
on toast, called in those days "Shit on a Shingle." Bicycle back, get into
the wet pads & jersey, out onto the field again. Gale strutting around as
we moved into tackle lines.

One afternoon, behind me: Velmar Clark, who was black. Our class
of '53 was the first one with blacks. Velmar I didn't know. The heat was
awful, my mouth bone dry. "No one ever drinks during practice," George
Gale had proclaimed.

Velmar reached down into his pants, into his jockstrap, & pulled out
a half-sucked lemon. He offered it to me.

I took it, sucked quickly, looked at Velmar &, glancing around,
handed it back to him.


I am proud that I did not refuse Velmar's lemon.

From time to time I wake up in the middle of night & revisit that
experience.

It happened so fast I had no time to think.

Maybe that is why it has haunted me for so many years, like a missing
angel.

# RADIO, WHILE COOKING

Art Tatum's Niagaran upsweep, his
   thoroughbred
stamina
        screens of tones eating
    tones in the pulsatile falls
      of man!


   Again & again:
stabbing for:  this fish, that fish—
   agami metronome!


     *Tatum,*
beyond belief,   dervish digitation
   tinkling kingdoms,  blind
         periscope—
star-burst cadenza quivers    harpsichordotic
   arrow spray.


You gotta hear him cutting out
   the viscera of dead pop
    American booty.

I have been shut down four months now,  *
blank patches during the day,
fragmentary dreams gone upon waking.
To watch & tend a beloved person suffering casts a net over
the subconscious hills & dales
where animals in combat with fabulous creatures
stir the moil that crystallizes into the language of the poem.
Dionysus, aged & bent, has been by my bedside.
Together we have prayed to Ariadne & to wounded Lascaux for Caryl.
His bent ram head, his tentaclesque "hands" I have held,
have smelled the hearth residue on his horns…
Has Ariadne heard? In Leningrad, 1987, I prayed to her to help me
recover lost luggage; minutes later a phone call from Pan Am:
the luggage had been found! Because I believe the practice of poetry
is action in the labyrinth, struggle at that bitter center, requiring
the clew of a feminine spirit, I have chosen Ariadne
as mistress elixir, with her candle burning through
the forests of webs & cul-de-sacs.


Lascaux is now
so wounded. What can one expect from this most holy site?
The passage from prehistory into history is an onslaught on
the analphabetic cascades of memory-entangled imagination.
I have the bird-headed man in my heart & believe
he hears, in bison paradise,
the cry of mental travel
manifest through the ages.


Best to respect the blank patches, & the failure of a single dream
to put its muzzle against my ear.
One must learn from one's being when it is shut down.
Such is the time when something may be coiling deep below…
Is it a Naga? A spirit snake trying to reach Caryl
with serum & bone-hardening relief?

We know no more than our ancestors at Lascaux about
the ornamentation of our fate.

8 June 2010

\*

The privilege of registering how much I care about you

& know that had you been less illness-driven
you might have made a unique art.

You have crucially aided me in many of my efforts,
have turned what energy & intelligence you can offer over to me,

to my work. Gesture of love, an offering beyond what
we can expect out of life. A weakened person giving

what she cannot give herself to another.
I write this now since I do not know to what extent

you will recover from your four kyphoplasties.
Oh I hope so much that you will!

Dear Caryl, all of us who know you are like
little fires placed about you.

16 December 2010

# OF A SWAN PALLID IN CIDER WASTES

Unsure of where I am, unplucked,
redolent with mortal caraway,
I steep in my own vaselinal integrity,
awaiting Popeye.
                    Why not? Who does death look like to you,
non-existent feeder?
                    Bitter pharmacological August
of a weird December,
                    December without spider,
June without loam. I am radiant with hopelessness
for the first time in my life.
                    What a lucky Palooka I was in Japan,
greatcoated with myth & the huge
                    interior coliseum of
the Blakean outlay. But I do not want to be back in Kyoto, I want
    to be where, meaning,
in the otherwise: the rootstock of my mind


Right now it is ambient rhinos pecking new-born
cleats, the no-one-home starkness
of a swan pallid in cider wastes. I feed this swan
an acorn taken from my sperm. It ignites,
exploding its own brothel of reserves.


What is it time to not do?


Should I dial Janis Joplin? Has she learned anything in death?


Or Lincoln? Or cousin Orville on our living-room davenport
pecking kissyface onto his girlfriend?


Memory is fracture, not the braking, but the lifting up
of cuts crisscrossing, dead-ending into view. I have so much
blank in my hold, so much

interstice, so much life lacunae, rain & fields of rats
listing, as if ships, in the pour of my
night-wrecked files.

Let's go, night companion, Yorunomado, dead head hunter
from a region known only to me & to Blake,  Let's go,
man I cannot talk to, let's whistle
to explain.

# CECILIA VICUÑA THREAD *

A blood clot is being absorbed by a russet's wandering fever.

Fraying loop hesitations are praying.

Thread as horizon-verticalized stamina.

Churned thread-furry whisper.

Totem-urgent beast tendrils: undertow against stasis.

Each milligram atick with spread-eagle crimson.

Heart's unsnarled artery argosy.

# BLACK JAGUAR  *

I am a crystal exposed to the true ones that inhabit the air.
I hear the sound of the steps of stones, of plants,
of things that human beings previously were.

My soul was carrying me as if I were its prey,
my body dangling from the claws of my soul…

When the envelope of words cracks, the water remains,
running & renovating itself unceasingly.
Words are live beings wandering on their own,
animals never resigned to a single skin.

Words couple like partridges. Words have descendants.

If I live only for myself, I have already chosen to die.

Poetry is the concrescent edge of a flat stone,
a needle that mends or tears.
It knows who says yes, who says no,
who is worthy of this life, deserves another, deserves none.

Without the black light of poetry,
I can't even make mistakes. I simply hit the target in reverse.

Night inseminated by a gull gives birth to lightning.

My head, full of sun sperm, bleeds crystalline blood.

I am the paw print in a rock, a million years old.

While the sound in my head turns into steady rain
I watch my name, *black jaguar,* emerge from the mirror.
It slowly corkscrews out, the writhing of precision
   as it meets time.

In memory of César Calvo

# THE LAVENDER FATHERS

I am one of the lavender fathers.


We want to find that Stone of Division
set as a corner in the human wall.
Our shoulders placed against it would set in motion
the transformation of temporality into great time.


Who you may ask are the lavender fathers?


We are the why & pale of anti-know.
We move inside the word wards of an original wetness,
measure veils stretched over bones.


Each word, a riddle of corridors,
is a capstone capping *sunyata*.


We once lived in the glyph balloons inhabiting Maya imagination.
Now we play, as if it were a cello, the Grünewald Isenheim Altarpiece,
drawing out its mole tones, its Sadean larvae...


Alas, we fathers are a mess. We've lost, out of our penises,
so much blood. Our ladies, from doing the thorn-pull,
speak to us only in shred-tongue, & while we are under all that occurs
we are weakened by non-existence.
We have lost our cohesive zap as sidereal gremlins,
we now only act up in metaphor...


And what does it mean to be lavender & not,
to be something emanating from an ancient moose,
the antler motion of a father, neck pouch as a bell,
an image of existence prior to being,
slicing lakes of light burgeoning into green hives, shadowed armatures,
hydromedusae sutra-stroking through world mind evolving.

# MEZCAL *

"cooked maguey"

9000 BC: we are told that they cut the flower stalk from the plant & sucked out its seed.

Once these plants are roasted, the "meat" is then carried to another pit, this one wood-lined & decorated with flowers. Like the umbilical cords of long dead people which were "planted" under the agaves, the meaty "bodies" of the agave are placed in the ground & water is added from a stream that flows off the slopes of Kweimarutse'e. As the roasted agave flesh ferments, this water is covered with foam that resembles clouds. The latter also refers to the souls of ancestors emerging like foam or vapor—once they have reached the sky, they will be able to trigger the rain that the community so dearly needs.

Mezcal, the spirit that simultaneously lashes us with its claws & rocks us to sleep.

When a Huichol fills his first gourd with this native spirit he pokes one finger into the vessel in order to sprinkle a few drops of its contents around him as a sacrifice to the dead, who crowd around him like eager children.

Mezcalnaut: one who uses mezcal to take a trip & does not get lost along the way.

If your partner cheats on you, drink mezcal. If you expect this to be the case, drink mezcal. If you are unfaithful, drink mezcal. If you have doubts, drink mezcal. At all times & in all circumstances, always drink mezcal. As the saying goes, when things go awry, drink mezcal. When things go well, drink some more.

# FOUND OBJECT

### For Richard Tuttle

1965, Lima, Peru: Barbara & I lived on a tiny street in the Miraflores district called Domingo Orúe. Barbara was nearing term with Matthew, & I was trying by hook or by crook to get access to the worksheets for César Vallejo's *Poemas humanos,* still in the clutches of Georgette de Vallejo. I often wandered out of our, by Peruvian standards, middle-class neighborhood into the "barriadas," where I observed a level of abject poverty I had not previously believed existed.

One morning, upon opening our door, I saw a discarded huarache in the street. The sole, cut from a chunk of car tire rubber, was worn so thin & run-over that it was more a part of the street than a sandal. Were I a Peruvian making art in Peru, I thought at the time, I would nail what was left of that huarache to the wall of an art gallery, a "found object," a mummy delicacy from that walker's life.

The rich are stacked like cordwood in that ex-wearer's soul. Barefoot, he wanders into the art gallery to collect all that is owed to him: his huaraches, the tire from which they were cut, the Cadillac, the landowner's plantation.

Dilemma of these post holes in the mind, whirlpool divinities sucking down, the rags of existence foaming high.

# SOME LADY  *

Adele Bloch-Bauer's gown with gold & azure
eye fish, her marmoreal chest
haloed by amoebic discs, "Starry
Night" & "Cosmic Superimposition" cartoons.

Her neck silver gripped,
her lips poised as if to utter mermaids.

Her mermaid-deprived lips,
her red lips alone below those Dormouse dormant eyes
while her fingers crinkle & fold,
while her fingers wonder:

"Do I Opheliaize in a pond of vertical money,
a marble-skinned socialite afloat in synthetic seeming,
a dunk of a dowager with body parts
peering through my clothing?"

Neue Galerie, NYC, 5 October 2009

# WOUND INTERROGATION *

In Matta's "Wound Interrogation,
a Malangganesque robot thrusts a flattened palm against
a large pulpy vaginal wound hung before it.
  Matta comments:
"The wound is separated from the human being & subjected to the
torture of intense examination by heinous machines. The bloody red
insides of the wound convey a life striving to exist, while the grays &
blacks of the demon robots remind one of an industrial plant."

This morning at the end of first light
the sky was drinking a sap so old I could hear the ayahuasca
cloud pythons gargling menstrual-seminal elixir.
I sensed the oracle gas between that Hadic distance &
Matta's robots interrogating—I propose: Persephone's sexuality.

Who exactly inhabits Hades' kingdom?

ALL DO (a chorus chants) THAT IS WHY HADES IS SO RICH

Can I interrogate this region of dense, cold air without light?

"You can, but my icy lace is blinding
& my knuckles, feeble from your Herculean viewpoint, are
hurricane poundings, tidal flail.
I am the dream jaguar which you created so as to, while
lurching out of bed, crash onto the floor.
I am the kobold which bit your ankle as you climbed out of a cave.
While you were driving home that night I bit again
so that you smashed into a ditch & broke that ankle twice.
I am, in other words, untapped center, shifty 'always.'
In my casket chloroform are blind troll suns, split
gourds of brain jam, simmering golden sweat known as world wars.
There never was a beginning!

All is nexus & midriff cast on an alabaster plain of marauding
tarantula-shanked camels..."

*

The frailty of being holed & rampant with closure.
Blake's angels feast on my neck
as strapped to this fuselage of honking verbs I watch Hades,
now a zyzzogeton, munching on alfalfa alpha.

For that matter, what is *deliverance?*
To find oneself present by Hades' cornucopian spread & grasp
that one must not mouth a single grape?

From her held-aloft bison horn the first Persephone squeezed time
& with that new periphery impregnated herself.

"Not to subject the change," Hades quipped,
"but what bugs you the most about America today?"

One: The suppression of the horrifying truth of the 9/11 assault (more
appropriately referred to as "The Pentagon Three Towers Bombing")
infests the American soul with a stifling sense of unreality charged by
the rivers of blood flowing alongside the Euphrates & Tigris through a
destroyed & failed state that may never again be reconstructed. I note
that otherwise responsible political thinkers like Oliver Stone & Bill
Maher will not even engage this ongoing nightmare.
    The truth of The Pentagon Three Towers Bombing is, like an undiag-
nosed plague, lodged in the American subconscious. This truth is now
the lie veneer of our dailiness. There is a knotted veil in our eyes building
rancor where there could be revelation.

Two: Since I have been writing, translating, & editing for over 50 years, I
have to deplore the degree writing programs that are in the process of
substituting creative writing for the art of poetry. In 1994 I wrote:

"Quotational Reality is the new Purgatory making each desire artificial."
My comment appears to identify Kenneth Goldsmith's aestheticized
plagiarism.

> Blankly while moonstruck egos immaculate at the verge
> poetry crawls into a curtained sty.
> The AWP floats a wreath over the death of depth.

The first poets, facing the incomprehensible division between what
would become culture & wilderness, taught themselves how to span it &
thus in such caves as Chauvet & Lascaux interrogate their situation. Our
key distinction may become that of being the first generation to have
written at a time in which the origins & the end of poetry became
discernable.

*

Dream is a fire burning alone out of contact with
the brushwood of my body.
I study it as Heraclitus studied gods endlessly changing soulscapes,
the squirrel face in a cloud simultaneously a fat weeping raccoon.
Sky stigmata. Archaic smile of the brave.
In the webs of Ananke the shaman struggles to vanish into
the dream flow of his avatar radiance.

An image is fire
around which language appears to be
tightly-packed ash.

James Hillman: "*I* and *soul* are alien to each other because of soul's
domination by powers, daimones and gods"

Soul is molten protocol.

Life is the blessing. Death the "less" in blessing:
Count Gaga spread-eagled & gagged in everyone's smoking gate.
Paul Valery's response: "I'm fucked & I don't give a fuck."

Humankind is timed, as if with a timer, by & for the apocalypse of
     immortality.
We are too far into that rage for, & range of, power versus the suicidal
hubris of millions willing to immolate to damage imperium & enter
their own immortality

Know thyself = know thyself to be mortal.

To think of the tethered mandala of the hand,
the radial glory of the fist unhooked from its fury.
Vallejo: "Our brave little finger will be big, worthy,
an infinite finger among the fingers."
Vodun thumb-post attended by 4 hexed dwarves.
Palm pressed to the Matta wound, to the Gargas wall:
new human negative: *the I am not    that is.*

I dream because I was born with hands.
And in dream tonight I held my fire in my hands,
my fire with Caryl's eyes!
Her dearest eyes peering out of my burning!

# TREE ROOTS AND TRUNKS   *

[Auvers, July, 1890]

And Persephone took Vincent's brush hand,
drawing him down to confront the fusion,
never achieved in painting, of the life of the world
& the inertia of the materials employed.

Her clitoris, when he dared to touch, felt triggerish.
If he could just release it as they tunneled & crawled,
would his mind let go of its descriptive miasma?
And form, of all the connective tissue with which it was stuffed?

Is this the eternity of finality, he wondered,
or the monadic demise of the moon?
Are these blue rootlets frisking about like snapped legs,
the motion within immobility?

A blue corm with three lidless eyes was staring at him,
a face now masked with twigs.
Is this my fix, Vincent puzzled, fumbling for that clitoral trigger...
am I just like a planet, or a paralyzed star?

The daily doldrums of only seeing what he knew,
only doing what he thought, having no right to do evil,
nearly always being alone, seemed to have paused....

As he continued to filibuster,
he realized that his eyes were filling with ants.
"The Great Transparent Ones," he thought
"communicate entirely through waves & odors...
The Great Transparent Ones...   undying ebb & flow...
the form the wind assumes in a cyclone,
the rays emitting light inside a bulb...

pillow of this dunghill…"

Vaginal blast of the son shot back.

For James Heller Levinson

# MICHAUX'S SIGNS   *

"The brush is done with.

The sovereign flow of ink seems audacious. Rather—because it is
somewhat slack in its flow—its barbarian black makes me audacious...

Bad black, black of refusal, of negation. Invader's black, crashing
through borders.

PAINT TO REPULSE!

Moreover, to repulse is also to extricate oneself, to break loose, to re-
cover one's liberty..."

"Signs, not of being complete,
but of being faithful to completion's transience,
not for conjugating, but for regaining the gift of tongues..."

      *

A spot gathering its measly strength to spread, to line-stain & fade.

Charming syncopation between these Acheulean scratchings &
    McClure's lion bellow fairs

"Prehistoire I": giraffe-like butchered soot stalking azure & yellow blasts.

Mescaline script: proliferation of corpuscular mite-like empty buds.

Your swaddling layer: tenacious & ever-deepening absence.

The sleeping excrement in the dreamer's hood.

Closed-eye vision: sensation of torsades twisting to fray.

Knots tightening into puddle-rubble mask collapses.

A mandala-mantic arachnid web-probing its prey.

Pale, glabrous, expressionless faces:
they know the Secret,
the awful Unnamable to whose underside all beings cling.

Based on an Acheulean incised ox rib, from between 200,000 and
300,000 years ago, a hominid appears to have made a curving slash, or
"core meander," then placed the cutting instrument on the slash & made
another curving cut, or "branch meander."

To find out for oneself. To find an out for self.

The perturbed objects of an upset taking its place.

Infinity at Combarelles: death as the core meander, life as the branch.

"Salads" of spilling overlays, coagulating, moldering…
or in Michaux's terms,
"movements of explosions, of refusal, of stretching every which way…"

"headless movements…
movements of folding and coiling up on oneself while expecting
    better…
movements of multiple spurts…
movements in place of other movements one cannot display but which
    dwell on the mind…"

Masticated muscles urinating music.

Shriveled umbilici knotted in prenatal hope

Structures turning into suture-gnarled wounds.

White floor ghosts, yes, that black-clad dancers host & fertilize.

Out of the population of the Beyond, soiled, marshy specters appear,
    rag bodies oscillating.

One noseless in sweet, questioning vacancy.
Another: from between half-blackened eyes, a skinny blood-stained
   elephant trunk descends.
A third whose face is scattered punctures.
A fourth: Michaux?
   Inspecting widower phantoms?


"Thy trillionic multitude of grahh, vhooshes, and silences.
   Oh you are heavier and dimmer than you knew
      and more solid and full of pleasure.
   Grahhr! Grahhhr! Ghrahhhrrr! Ghrahhr. Grahhrrr.
Ghrahhrr-grahhhhrr! Ghrarrrr. Gahrahhrr Ghrahhhrrr.
   Ghrarrr. Ghrahhr! Ghrarrrr. Gharrr. Ghrahhhrr.
      Ghrahhrr. Ghrahr. Grahhr. Grahharrr. Grahhrr."


And now for a Basho "frog leap" improvisation:
   White space   ah—
      black ink!
   Presensed presence


During the Marie Chouinard Compagnie performance of *Mouvements,*
eight dancers dropped,   bunched,   then
            in peristaltic agitation,
caterpillared wickedly across the stage.


Daddy-long-legs line body with multiple thread-like meandering
   appendages.


Searching for a brail trail in a jungle of groping.


Whiteness routed, twenty capilliform illegibles seize control of their
   page space.


No ending but ongoing tentacles wandering thwarted fusion,

"the scabbard torn off, one is somebody else
any somebody else
no longer to pay tribute
a corolla opens, bottomless dive…"

The primal dance of biota disobeying form, divvying up the void spoils,
    the splatter-rich blocked escapes.

# LISTENING TO BEETHOVEN IN OUR PRIUS

Inner balance suddenly tuned to
the head of John Kennedy singing in the Huron River,
his assassins, their heads likewise appear,
cursing, crowing, Hoover & Johnson, their heads,
Oswalds popping up everywhere—
Beethoven's 31st in 2010, played by Pollini,
pistons pumping *give him reprieve, give him never*
(I was driving home from the fish market)
semi-final annihilatude of ax-like chords
Oh! I'd like to leave poetry with that NO NO NO NO
cast into the hellbroth of the heart!

# FULCRUM

> "Lean lean on the abyss on vertigo
> lean lean on nothingness
> lean lean on conflagration"
> —Aimé Césaire

I lean on a white salmon & cream-colored Arachne sending out her lasso
over the bright patio of La Pescalerie.

On Whitman's "kelson," the backbone of Osiris indicated along the
bottom of the coffin against which the mummy's spine pressed.

On the Sheela-na-gigs, like tots in a green glade, dancing the Formorian
jig.

On my bottle of one-thousand-proof uterine grog.

On every angel's insectile feelers.

On the Abbé Breuil—unlike Ezekiel lying in dung to raise man to a
vision of the infinite—on his back below the ceiling of Combarelles
tracing the silex sortilege.

On Stevens' "vast ventriloquism of sleep's faded papier-mâché."

On the breath-favorable Sabbath moment in every hour.

On the slave-strewn harpsichord I discovered in my mother's womb.

On the Lima "barriadas" when, starting to think politically,
    February 1966, right after Matthew was born,
I climbed those awful hills of waterless poverty
in a fantasy that I was following some terrible new Stations of the
Cross...

Absence as the unacknowledged genuflection in every breath—
I bow to you, O primary presence for billions of years.
Bow back to me, gaseous nebulae, so beautiful, so null!

Beyond memory and experience to hear a mole orchestra
    knocking out Beethoven.
To hear in that clangor the cut-up breasts of slaughtered women being
    reformed into incendiary grenades.

I lean on the madness & the necessity of pulling their pins.

# BODHISATTVA REMAINS    *

For Mary Heebner

Bodhisattva A: this meditating figure destroyed by
rampaging 18th century Burmese brutality.
Crossed legs now support a blown-apart torso.
(Vallejo's Venus de Milo: the damaged one truer than the complete?)
Rising off the remaining platforms
stumps float a void, inverted broken hammers.
Ayutthaya is a wound issuing a thousand streams.

Bodhisattva B: why did the Burmese leave the crossed legs,
destroy just heads & torsos? Curious plant forms,
gibbous posts, as if the practice of meditation
supports rapine configurations.
As if meditation circles about a wagon-jammed center.
Meditation as scouts on horseback
circling enwalled pioneers. Circumference-invaded center.
The mind in hatchet to itself.

Bodhisattva C: chest halved, side
a precipice, as if one might climb into neckless light—
light without jugular flow
light as headless sheen.

Bodhisattva D: crossed legs on warped platter.
"*Sunyata* is served." War as the anti-raga of love.
We live in a fugal meadow/abattoir:
the lover's tears scarlet with tinged prescience of
what's to come. Iraqi marketplace, 2007:
explosives-loaded Down Syndrome girls
pushed like blind animals into the crowd.

# STEVENS AT TENOCHTITLAN    *

The Great Temple of Tlaloc & Huitzilopochtli. I wonder how long I would last at Tenochtitlan. I am looking at Huitzilopochtli in his feathered blue hummingbird headdress seated at the top of the 180 foot high pyramid. He is wearing a mantle of rich green feathers adorned with gold. In his left hand he carries a white shield with five tufts of white feathers arranged in the form of a cross. In his right hand the god holds a staff in the form of a snake, all blue & undulating. He is shod in blue sandals. Before him four priests—smeared black with bitumen, white circles around their mouths—have spread-eagled a Tecali prisoner of war on the sacrificial stone block, each holding an arm or a foot. A fifth priest has placed a snake-shaped yoke on the prisoner's throat. The high priest now thrusts his flint knife in a long sweep down from the prisoner's breastbone to the base of his stomach &, reaching into this gash with a dexterous twist, tears out his heart. After raising it to the sun, the high priest throws the steaming heart into Huitzilopochtli's face. The cadaver is then rolled down the steps of the pyramid where it is retrieved by its owner—the soldier who captured the prisoner—carried away, cooked & eaten.

John Lash: "With their uncanny sense for the transposition of twinning powers, the Aztecs place the image of their Flayed God, Xipe Toltec, on the *inner face* of a ceremonial mask: so that the priest who wears the mask must literally face the sacrificial double as he dances, blind, in the flayed skin of the sacrificed victim. While the mask mouth screams in silent agony, Xipe Toltec blows the sacred current of somatic force (*mana, Ehecatl*) directly into the third eye of the celebrant."

Hands of a sacrificed hang like gloves next to those of a priest.
Ragged skin ends across his back are laced together with cords.
The priest wears this "skin costume" for 20 days.

"The stale grandeur of annihilation."    Stevens at Tenochtitlan.
Think of him there, in tweeds before a skull-rack,
thinking: "This is a confirmation of life as it is not.
Why have I wasted my time on insurance?

I could have been a rattlesnake in a grand stone labyrinth
zigzagging to the sound of heart-rip...
I was wrong to write Latimer in 1938 that life in Mexico was without
    thesis.
Indeed, these Aztecs are thesis-possessed. Where else is fulfillment:
to die & to be eaten as the 'rep' of a god?
They rule, the priests interpret, interpose, the people obey.
Symbiosis of god and man.
Man on the pulley of the sun.
No soft emotionalism here!"

Eternity as a feathered rattlesnake. Eyeless sockets staring out of stone at
the eagle vessel each heart is to be burned in. No compassion,
no possibility of a Greek "escape." No economics,
just these chest-mined adorations. Your raddled fate.
Absolutes without lantern.

Stevens at Tenochtitlan. Thousands of skulls threaded on poles.
The black cavities of their orbits, nasal apertures: marks on infernal dice.

According to Aztec religion, man has no other aim on earth but to feed
the Sun with his own blood, without which the sun will die of exhaus-
tion. This tragic dilemma obliges him to choose between participating in
massacres or bringing about the end of the world.

At Tenochtitlan, we might have grasped the mantis imperative:
penis still in female as she relieves us of our heads.
Blackened-blood-scabbed "god actors" (more intimate with the people
than with their own families) slash their penises down the middle to
    become impotent
(so as to not offend the gods).

In 1519, 371 towns were paying tribute to Tenochtitlan.
Cortez saw 136,000 skulls deposited in The Great Temple.

The Aztecs were victims of what Weston La Barre calls an archosis: "a massive and fundamental misapprehension of reality often of incalculable antiquity culturally."

What is *our* archosis?   Again, La Barre:
"Since all thinking men now face the same terror—the extinction of our species—they may grudgingly attend to such a thesis that wars depend to an alarming degree on the treacherous holy fantasy (false but insatiably desired) of individual immortality and on each man's denied oedipal murderousness."

Tlaloc was worshipped as God of Rain, Lightning, Thunder and Thunderbolts. He was venerated & feared throughout the entire land. No other idol was more adorned or enriched with stones & splendid jewels. His feast fell on the twenty-ninth of April & people came from all parts of the land to commemorate it.

Just after dawn the kings & lords with their followers took a six year old child & placed him within an enclosed litter so that he would not be seen. When they arrived before the image of the god Tlaloc, the child was killed. Then King Motecuhzoma together with all his great men & chieftains approached the idol & presented finery & a rich garment to the god. When the stews, breads & chocolates had been put in place, the priests who had slit the child's throat appeared with his blood in a small basin. The high priest wet the hyssop which he held in his hand in that innocent blood & sprinkled the idol along with all the offerings & food. And if any blood was left, he went to the idol Tlaloc & bathed its face & body with it. If the blood of that child was not sufficient, one or two other children were killed to complete the ceremony.

Coatlicue, yes. The suspicion that in our hearts snakes are kissing snakes.

The knowledge that down our backs we trail a heart & hand lopped headdress.

That we move encumbered by all that our races have not only lived through but done.

So imagine your mind, write down the imbrication, & kiss your sweetheart goodnight—knowing that the Aztecs are still steering their skull plows through our brains.

# CYLINDER IDENTITY

Walt Whitman's last words recalled as I shift onto
my left side, pillow stuffed between knees.
Warry Fritzinger was Walt's last nurse,
& at the poet's request would turn him in bed.

Are there left side dreams? Right side ones?
Does the heart under right side pressure
contract differently than when the left side is raised?
Are dreams position oriented?

An Eden of sorts
seems to spread out below the circular
causation of the dream, all the animals in pause,
holding their breath not for me,
but to see what dictates dreams ray down…

"Warry, shift," Walt muttered,
&, as he was turned, entered that nearby
mausoleum underworld with his rained-on name.

Whitman shifts occasionally in my dreams,
a thousand-year-old man; instead of hands, talons—
which I read as the hunger of a Sudanese child.
Old old Walt, with floating Cro-Magnon braids,
& wisps of scimitars,
& elk fuzz, owl roostings,
all this roasted plenitude a part of my
cylinder identity.

    Snow     aerial
  hourglass


The soda fountain of the sky is seltzering!
Overarching Nut   working both paps!

Down-light, they
   touch down,
                    dendritic crystals
needle-locking.
            I think of the precisely fitted
      cyclopean stones of
Sacsahuamán—
                 the flutter stasis of the weighted & the weightless
                     in mental sublimation


        Albication of the front walk, the bordering grass
   albescent


        Inch deep angel forest


                                27 December, 2010

# PAREIDOLIA

Around 4 A.M. this winter I often get out of bed, pee, and then
standing by our bathroom window
look through the leafless branches of our front yard red maple
which demethodize the two main door lights of
The First United Methodist Church of Ypsilanti across the street,
turning them into eyes watching me through the mass of twig-barbed
    spear-like branches pointing every which way…

The strangeness of this branch-constructed countenance
evokes an *axis mundi* specter, or
Yggdrasil after Odin hung from it for nine days…

As I continue to stare, Hart Crane's suicide
—suddenly now identified as a "sorghum suicide"—passes through…

How close we are at all points to the sources that spellbind
    our psychic reality.

Is this church-eyed branch mingle a face of night?
Or night playing with my eyes as I filter
God adoration through
a maple tree's pagan fate?

Each tree is a world tree whose roots engrail
the barnacled scoria of the haul.

2015

# AT THE BRITISH MUSEUM, 11 APRIL 2007

That anything archaic exists today
attests to erasure's unbowed adversary.

How do I know this perforated antler from La Madeleine
   is alive?
Because, half-buried in it, a horse is emerging,
eye holes filled with ochre,
a dream of ornamental blood.

How do I know I am alive?
Because, half-buried in me, my death is cross-legged on
  a cattail mat,
vertical carrion with illicit halo.

                 Sift
        of biotics
            open to

  faith in the sun lathe
around which the rasp of mortality is grating
a microscopic tundra scene.

       Leaf-thin
disc escape,    to wear it
             in my throat.

           For Pierre Joris & Nicole Peyrafitte

# LES EYZIES, JUNE 2008   *

A viper sheep head in the rock face
    (behind a boarded-up house
  on Rue de la Préhistoire)
right eye a furrow——Çatalhöyük hybrid!

The "speech" of this crag, its silent, prayerful snooze

How I am designed, sized, by what underlies.
                The last time here?
*The* weight in my heart throughout this cave tour.
Here three decades ago I descended into the primordial underworld.

Starlings in flutter explore the viper sheep head.
Having walked so often below this crag to the old museum's
  "power room,"
to stand below, on this street, now. And to acknowledge, once again,
the Upper Paleolithic's reshaping of my life...
      Ah, lenient atmosphere...
Breath-favorable sabbath of those hours...

To be simultaneously in the present & the deep past,
& for several minutes to be the humble attendant of
  a viper sheep head altar.
To be vertical    until the Vézère
      pulls me home.

# THE HORN OF TIME

Bergman's "Wild Strawberries"—
high on a town wall, a clock with no hands
confronts the old doctor as if
he is lost to time.
                    In my case, the hands,
having left the clock face, are drifting about in the air,
sort of playing tag.

Caryl's vertebral fractures have loosened me from my self.
Right now no dream twin times me.

The clock hands are signing, as if I were deaf,
an altered semantics of time.

What can faceless Laussel,
scraped clean of green immersion,
tell us about the horn of time?

Is time the emptying of the animal horn?

Is planetary peril inscribed at image's origin?

Does Laussel hold aloft the notched
i.e., timed, larval
carnality of this foreboding?

# THE JOINTURE    *

For Herbert Lust

[1]

Imagination is the keelson of paradise.
The Maya, the Aztec & the Asmat entwine my I-beam.

Step up onto the serpent throne. God K'awil is present:
his left foot a fer-de-lance whose jaw-sprung head wears
a gorgeous myth-scrambled headdress, birth cord tucked inside.
My mother's vagina is a simulacrum of K'awil's open maw.
Emergence to this world infused with Gladys's veins
braided with those of her three sisters, Georgia, Ruth, & Mary,
a quartet of visionary anacondas, each in dread-holy robes.
When I signal them they turn into beavers,
barking & flashing their gate-like tails.

The essence of imagination: access to one's own penetralia,
one's inner wilderness, its atavistic hosts.
Looking through the vehicular cinders of night's telescope
I am a 12 year old Asmat sucking off a 16 year old,
caught up in the pistons of a drive
to wear a semen bone through my nose,
to be vermilion in a cloud of gnats,
to kill to amass the soul strength of others,
to dine on brain marrow for male power.

[2]

The men's house is a structure stolen from the moon's iced
glades, a seclusion
banked against the dread of female play,
a "between" where the adults are bannered worms,
incandescent, organ

opulent, skulls loaded with priceless marrow
or, in the case of the adolescents,
hungry for insemination, &
when Indianapolis teenagers,
singing loudly, after football practice, in the shower,
"Goodnight Irene, I'll see you in my dreams."
This is a structure firmly in place as
the poltergeist of war. Men huddle in
a Washington stadium of antique rage at what they are:
needy melons forever seeking prime.
Isolation is the diamond gore. Bring in
the crocodile. We want to fondle her mildewed tresses.
Decorated skulls are vitality transmitters
wedged in the novices' groins.
Just how big is the mens' house? It is an archetypal
separation continuum operative in all tiers:
Phil Delta Theta & Enola Gay over Asmat mud,
a vast humming concourse of insect sentience.
The young are layered dream flavors,
ventriloquistic
trophies in the underworld desire to flood the world.


[3]


September 21, 2011, Bud Powell's birthday:
a dragon of morning glories surges our wire-mesh fence,
spilling onto the pavement *Ipomoea violacea* blooms.
They twine upon themselves, twisting twins twisting,
as an imago emerging from a cocoon.
                              *Ipomoea:*
Fr. Gr. *ips, ipos,* a kind of worm + *homoios* like

A vision raved by Xochipilli,
        a "god of flowers, in statued stone,"
mask eye holes aligned with eyeless sockets
described by Hart Crane as "sweet eye-pit basins."

Psilocybin caps, morning glories, sinicuichi, poyomatli
carved in bas-relief on his torso, legs, arms, & head.
"Absorbed in *temicxoch*," which Gordon Wasson translates as
"entheogenic ecstacy," Xochipilli rears back on his plinth,
shuddering, grimacing. His hands which may have,
     in Aztec time,
held bunches of psilocybins, are poised, half-cupped.


[4]


What does it mean to see with the eyes of the soul?

To witness oneself emerging from one's cocoon
as *Ipomoea* emerges from its uterus of vines
to glory in the morning sun?

Xochipilli rocking on his psychoactive throne, sparkling
with emptiness lightning, "drinks the sun."

Is death a return to a nebula atmosphere in which we are
encindered & rebaptized as fetal charred extinctions?
To be an extinction! To horripilate in gas choirs boiling with nothing,
radiant with No, & in No—what to find?

A purse empty with a velvet forever?

Is the concept of the holy locked into our corollaceous abyss?


[5]


Tonight I have placed my mother's bones in anatomical position.
In her skull I have imagined the torn web of self.

     Tjurunga, impinge,
open your foramen magnum to me.

Let me taste male *muelos,* know it as closely
as the worms swarming, exposed while clearing autumn leaves.
Once these bones were arranged,
I ate the guardian spider who offered herself to me.
I ate her carbon mask too. But first I severed her legs,
then drained her spinnerets. Each of her eight eyes shone.

My worms now advance, waving their antlers,
each of which drools a Ganges from its tines.

[6]

Imagination is the truth. And I am brought home
from the Methodist Episcopal Hospital,
a wee tot, to North Delaware Street, June 13th, 1935.
My mother is 37, my father 40.
For years they've tried to have a baby, & here I am,
like a gnome discovered in a serpent's gullet,
or a red-headed imp called "Sonny" prancing in the tub.
They coo & babble at me to elicit something from themselves,
unaware that in their still unsounded souls is the shadow
clash of ancestors only imagination can tap.

At thirteen days my tail is still in my mouth
an uroboric memory: being folded inside self,
fertilizing self, squealing at self, barking up my shadow,
a palindrome crawling back forwards.

Father is a baleful shark eye rimmed with fire.
Father is a horse-headed ant. Father listens to my every sound
encouraging his "Little Sicker" to pluck a natal bouquet of budding coos.
I am a beet, my cranium is fuming, my fontanel still ajar,
which means: I may never be fully fledged… Fine,
                    as along as I am fully born!

Imagination is the jointure.
At the crossroads of Rumsfeld & Yorunomado
souls clash in a superfetation of greed & power,
as if there were immunity from death,    so cunningly
is the worm of mortality disguised as a steadily flickering star.

Maya imagination & Iraqi catastrophe: my Clashing Rocks.

[7]

FIRST BEING

*Stone spoke fire    spoke rain    stone*
*moved below, an under-all*
*rhyming with animal tone—*
*stone as well spoke death.*
*Many assembled humbly before it*
*believing it might bridge the distance between*
*primal sea & bottom mud.*
*Creature after creature dove down,*
*Mr Crab   Mr Bear   Ms Leech*
*pebbles in their mouths as offerings*
*to see if bottom was endlessness upended*

*They scraped up a little mud,*
*brought to surface creational mail!*

*This "cosmic dive" may have been a Cro-Magnon myth.*
*People went down into the caves*
*as if into an endlessness to work with*
*the equivalent of bottom mud—*
*they confronted stone,*
*flattened a hand against a wall,*
*spat manganese or ochre around this outstretch,*
*then removed it*

*leaving a "hand" without a hand:*
*negation's first*
*hand-shaped presence*

Is Gilgamesh the end of the "cosmic dive"? He dives for
a vigor-restoring plant, pulls it up, brings it back.
While he sleeps the serpent soon to meet Eve
steals this prize to renew its own life.

*Here are the hands my mother formed.*
*All of my fingers flex a given giving,*
*a wandering improvisation on the given*

The jointure. And the kaleidoscopic legacy of Coatlicue's
extraordinary womb, where Yorunomado & I, snug in our bliss sacs,
listen to Powell improvise on "being".

*In Creedmore asylum, Bud sketched a keyboard*
*on his cell wall so as to hear*
*if only in his own mind*
*improvisation's handless presence.*

[8]

Is there a "once upon" when time did not exist?  Does the lack of
narrative in most Cro-Magnon imaginings indicate that animals &
human being were not perceived as being part of what we would call a
background?

To be or not to be may be the question, but to be & not to be may really
be the burden. The creation of an image in cave dark must have enabled
the power of not being to compete cogently with being. The bison on the
wall, in flickering hand-lamp-fire, was possibly more real in non-being
than the living beast.

*To look without understanding.* E.M. Cioran writes that this is paradise. To be penetrated by the observed which enters one & goes on through one—without one.

No progress, no damnation, no pockets into which to put the tidal coiling in & out of feelings. No explanations. Just the blunt force of survive powering through, disappearance its yoked mate.

A silence older than being. The sound of nothing     doing.

Basis of the "hidden wealth" of Hades:  the fullness of the void experienced not as absence but as hidden presence to be drawn forth as the animal matrix one is exiting.

[9]

The New Guinea Asmat believe that no one dies a natural death. To avenge the dead killed in combat or by black magic, they carve banyan trees into stacked ancestor figures. These ceremonial poles, which also commemorate the first Asmat woodcarver hero Fumeripits, are set up in villages to assuage the anger of the dead, especially those killed in headhunting raids.

A banyan tree to become a ceremonial pole is hunted, killed, uprooted & stripped of its bark (releasing a bloodlike sap). All of its roots are cut off except for the plank or buttress root. Turned upside down after being carved, the pole now has the buttress root at or near the top. This root, carved into an open scrollwork, is called a "tjemen," meaning: penis, canoe prow, pennant. The model for the poses assumed by the carved ancestor figures making up the pole is the praying mantis (a symbol of headhunting, based on the female's decapitation of the male after mating).

The tjemen actually begins right above the penis of the top body on the pole (the "soft" penis is quite visible in its correct anatomical position) & projects outward from the ancestor stomach. Carved into the scrollwork are little humanoid figures, or symbolic flying foxes or praying mantises. The tjemens evoke not only penes but thrusting, pointed pregnant bellies. As such, they seem to me to be unique undifferentiated pregnancy claims, expressing the urge to be phallic & female, with their origins probably in prehistory: primal, androgynous presences.

[10]

[Standing before the ancestor poles in the Michael Rockefeller Wing of the NYC Metropolitan Museum]

## ASMAT ENIGMAS

*Out of the lower gut*
*the mantic prayer for gestation, to bear progeny in*
*the phallic push into the pregnant*
*abyss of the mystery of male birthing.*

*Non-existent gestation,*
*the egg pregnant with the maggot of self,*
*lifting high my ancestor beak of creation,*
*on whose shoulders do*
*I stand, Asmat Yorunomado,*
*Asmat spirit vine, World Tree of*
*ancestor on ancestor, pushing out breech-*
*birthed brethern, O*

*where   are   the   sisters?*
*Don't ask Asmat man.*
*Tall morgue of male perpendicularity, touching*
*sky, mud,   tree man:  mangrove*
*root of my ancestor hole*
*filled with fellow brains, fellow semen—*

*Who is that homunculus*
*ready to pop out the tip of our push?*

*Is he the mantis man to be born*
*who will decapitate our enemies so that*
*from their brain bowls*
*we may drink*
*a magisterial maggot brew?*

[11]

Phi Delta Theta "hell week," 1954: I was made to wear a bull's dick
around my neck to class. Tonight I'm looking at a painting of an Egyptian
pharaoh. He has a bull's tail hanging out of his royal kilt. Or is that a
bull's dick? Or the umbilicus of his soul Double?

The rupture of the human from its natural origins forever to be
unrealized?

During my self-initiation (Kyoto, 1963),
Yorunomado was unlocked from the literality of my guts.
He said: "I will now insert new guts in you,
labyrinth coils to indicate that you have, via my emergence,
visited pregnant Coatlicue's urn, where her beheaded body was stuffed,
that you be witness to her magical corpse
out of which twin rattlesnakes ascended.
Once above the urn's rim, they swerved to kiss. The jointure.
When you look through my eyes
you will notice goddess Coatlicue looks at you through
one rattler's left eye, the other rattler's right eye,
*the Aztec veil.*
                    The goddess form is terrible
because sacrifice *is* her animated base.
Her face *is* the rattlesnake amor within man."

[12]

Dream, November 15, 2010: I return to my apartment shared with others to find that all has changed: my things are missing as if swallowed up in a redo involving not only curtains & added rooms but density, *thingness,* as if the walls are now padded with cloths & boards. As I search for what is mine the density increases, *as if to search means to densify.* There is no goal or end to my search, only thickening obstruction, a womanless harem of garments, draperies, rooms packed double & triple fold. I am emptiness at the mercy of thingness, with place folded in & over me as dream awareness without identity or mercy.

Here I note that the poet as a densifier (German word *Dicht* ("dense," "thick," "tight")) occurs both in *Verdichtung* (Freud's term, "condensation") & in *Dichtung* ("poetry"), *Dichter* ("poet").

James Hillman: "Each dream is a child of Night, affiliated closely with Sleep and Death, and with Forgetting (Lethe) all that the daily world remembers. Dreams have no father, no call upward. They come only from Night, and they have no home other than in the dark realm… Amor, wings folded, his torch pointing down…"

> In the bitter conflict at that mantic center
> where intercourse is beheading, I turn into a moth
> baled in the silk of the space in my flame.

> And sleep is dyed by what the water in my body remembers.

[13]

Dark red, water-worn ironstone cobble
found in the South African cave of Makapansgat.
Australopithecine, they say, about three million years old
with gouged eye & mouth holes.

Think of it as the first bowling ball, three holes: finger grips.

What is it to roll what will become the head of Orpheus down a lane?

To project one's mind down a single blame?

Dear tomb alert, I am at pause with your epigenetic furrow.

[14]

The anima flees, and the ghosts of riven sheep
coagulate in memory's occluded ravine.

Is there a core portal?

I will not forgive Indianapolis for
the torture of Sylvia Likens. Below the surface of the city Gene Krupa
called "a beautiful graveyard" was racism & horrible rectitude.
James Whitcomb Riley lurching down his boarding house hallway
drunk on rhyme maidens plastered among the daffodils.

[15]

The "Venus" of Hohle Fels, some 37,000 years old,
is a kind of telescopic microscope. Her mammoth ivory surface,
tobacco-brown, is a hive abuzz with self's odious organ feasts.
She is 2.4 inches tall, but her compacted energy is so dense
she is as commanding as Coatlicue. Were I, eyes closed,
to run my fingers about her body I imagine that I would feel trails
marked by hooves, paws, feet & dragged remains.
As I mentally palpitate her gnarled pudendum,
a fetal shiver draws my hand across the open eyes of twins...

The jointure. Maybe I should dial Yorunomado.
Surely he will have some salubrious flexibility to contribute.
Hey, Night Window, what's up?

"I've just come from a concert in the subconscious Everglades
where I listened to Elizabeth Bishop's angel,
a fourteen foot croc, sawing away on a shipwrecked viola.
And you?"
          While you were speaking, I was visited by
a demon beaver who smacked up into me the Charleston of
an ever-cresting dam. I scrawled in a book of leeches
miraculous cant, signs of limes & waifs, terms unknown to the elect.
My book kept filling with preps & surgery,
my back split open to reveal its spider math, veins green with Adam,
a paradise of lateral vises, reigns & falls of organs
so powerful I could only dance. I was *under* rock, of rock, speaking rock
out of an age I was growing into as I grew out.


          Yorunomado: "I woke up within your Charleston
to discover that the dream body weighs thousands of tons.
Tried to move my arms, my legs,
they were massive forevers with an inertia unmovable.
Do you know anything about the mentality of that fearsome weight?"


It's very ancient, I think.
Tied into animal loss.
Gilgamesh again.
We are told that as Enkidu penetrates Shamhat, the beasts reject him.
As the gazelles move away, Enkidu's legs refuse to move.
He could not run as he had before. Now we are told he had *reason* &
    *broad understanding*..
Animal loss.
The weight of primal separation, forever.
There's more: as you dream, Yorunomado, burdened with your massive
    forevers, Shamhat opens her muzzle around your head & blows.
Her breath, once interpreted by Enkidu's now differential mind as *every-
    man is my potential foe because I have had intercourse with a woman*,
is interpreted by your mind as *all human intercourse is with the mother*.
The Enkidu-Shamhat coupling brought intimate allegiance into the
    human sphere.

As Enkidu entered the separation continuum, men to come were *released*
from the animal womb.
A gain for civilization? Perhaps.

At the same time: the fuse that detonated into war.

Our dream weight is now intensified by war's religious goal:
an apocalypse of the earth turned inside out
not to realize Jerusalem but to achieve
an immortality sty of roving worms & lakes of fire.

   [16]

*Imagination,*
  *the great loosener,*
  *imaginal love,*
  *religious nature without religion,*
*walks a blind-folded plank,    steps off*

"I have many body parts,
& so I live simultaneously in many zones.
Beyond conscious unity, I am a traveling labyrinth of octocameral
tentacles bearing eyes, a bittersweet center underscored by
arachnoid mating & minotaur wedlock.
The female masticates the head of the male as he makes
a night deposit on her seminal receptor.
The head of Orpheus aslit & porous to the fin-handed leech queen
percolating his brain coral with servings of menstrual mud.
A Morpho on morphine a morphology of musical mayhem.
The impossible as alive as a millipede in furl with its scurry.
Memory is fracture, dead-endings crisscrossing into view.
I have so much blank in my hold, so much interstice,
so much life lacunae, rain & fields of rats listing,
as if ships, in the pour of my night-wrecked files".

Animals painted on Upper Paleolithic cave walls are Cro-Magnon's alter-
  egos,
'alter' as in 'other,' the *nagual* or animal aspect.


                    Earlier it was asked:
'What does it mean to see with the eyes of the soul?'


To witness one's imago emerge as image,
art in its final adult, sexually mature, & usually winged state.


  [17]


And suppose we do crack that anti-safe of anti-safes, the abyss?


Will the Enkidu-Shamhat tragedy become a post-*hagazussa* comedy,
old witch flights off that fence separating wilderness from culture
  being replaced by
virtual humankind's cybernetic swarming of the remains of becoming
  & self-exploration by
ersatz immortalities discovered in the cut-loose shadow of the self?


Learning to milk oneself is the next to impossible mining.


To live rigorously with the strata-fired continuum of the moment,
with the ochre of farraginous dreams, with the vitriol of
  no always no never—
blind to my own dimensions but determined to not *misknow*
what sets me outside myself,   Cro-Magnon Asmat Xochipilli
opened by the sun to reveal the mantic mantis man
sprouting out of the ipomoeic
        eclosion in his Pan chromatic cocoon.

# NESTED DOLLS   *

In Memory of Kenneth Warren

Inside Mitt Romney: Paul Ryan.
Inside Paul Ryan: Ayn Rand.
Inside Ayn Rand: William Edward Hickman.
Inside William Edward Hickman:
    the dismembered body of Marion Parker.


Coatlicue within *Coatlicue*   again & again.


Lady Xoc pulling a thorn-studded rope through her perforated tongue
—as a spider transforms its netted prey into liquid
(one might say the spider drinks its witness)
so did the Maya burn blood-spotted fig bark strips to hallucinate double-
    headed Vision Serpents in order to glimpse in twining fumes
the blood reciprocity between gods & humankind.


The Irish Sheela-na-gig with grotesque lower abdomen, cavernous oval-
    shaped vulva, held-open, so big as to reach the ground.
Sheela's genital areas were rubbed (like the yonis of Hindu goddesses).
Birthing stones may have been placed in her genitals.
Sheelas were drilled, head & body, with holes, portrayed in vertical
    birth-giving posture.
Some have protruding amniotic sacs or vertical channels cut below the
    vulva, egg-shaped objects lying between their open legs.
Hanging between the open legs of the Romsey Sheela:
a baby's head with eyes, nose, & mouth.

Is there an Irish god of death?
There must be, & at 1200 AD Sheela-na-gig must be his bride.
It is her knob-faced sickle-shadow in reburgeoning oaks.
Her ribs bear breast paws.
Bishop's whore. Lich gate. Hole.
Dyadic apotropaion.
Compounded with negation, Sheela affirms.


So, what is image? The mage in I?
An imago charged with pupa karma?


Image is the reality of the invisible world.


Reflected in every image:
the labyrinth underlying the poem,
the spider web underlying the labyrinth.


Enghosted in every image: Minotaur & spider.


There has only been one real change: the appearance of being.


As if the night itself is sarcophagus
& we: sleepers in pause between closed-eye vision
& primordial remove.


Absence, the weightless boulder upon which I broods.


Because of nothingness we desire to bloom.

When I view a Munch painting, I am facing Edvard's soul. Morbid, but it
is Edvard's, & compared to America in the world it is lividly affirmative.
The courage of this forlorn Norwegian a hundred years ago to confront
the lineaments of melancholia. O deep good blackness in the heart!


In the void of exhaustion: the costumes of dreams.


A 19th century Nigerian man with seeds for eyes,
blackness intensified by leatherine pomade.
He shines, a crater, in a socket set in the void,
wild as that glowing abyss in the Milky Way.


Beautiful to live in this brief gratitude of bone
on loan from my Cro-Magnon Hadic layer.


As a dreamer I'm a Cubistic portrait of my ego.
The Theater of the Egg.
Tonight, after Whimpy on Maldoror, a mosquito will hum Mozart,
the Egg director channeling the cicatricle dictation.


There may be one door, Robert Kelly, that cannot be opened:
the Sibelius sarcophagus, or
the Sibelius parasympathetic symphony:
bone flute at 35,000 B.P.
Joyous hollow trill of movement below the egg.


In Blake's thought
there is mighty womb bliss / consternation.
Creation & the Fall signal expulsion into life outside.

Blake's ambivalence toward the feminine is based on vaginal exit.
                    The crisis!
And if "crisis cult" is fundamental to religion,
human being is imbued with crisis sensibility.


The father bellows if not punctured becomes savior breath


To be fully born: to take responsibility for an emergence
     accountable to mortal synthesis.


Born our lives are twilight contoured.
We emerge at 1 P.M., the sun already descending.
We are the tiny mountain behind which it sets.
We are the tramontation.
                    We do not slip the caul.
We are capped—calotte—our helmet is occult.
It will take apocalypse to slip the network. But what
          will be uncovered?
Will the revelation be, in flesh & in syntax,
that the bulk of our existence has been invisible?
That in psyche we had twigs, branches, growing
               out the back of our skulls,
that all of us were wearing feather-massive, ground-trailing
          war bonnets?


There was no war until there were city states capable of God formations.
With such formations arose the desire for immortality,
     generated by the immortality archetype,
with this correlative: one must kill—to provide soul food for the dead—
     to become immortal.

Kafka & Escher: Siamese twins connected by a mirror.


The big crude Wall Street sign "Jump You Fuckers" made me think:
McCain jumped. And was tortured.
Can a tortured man be trusted as President?
The hand on the red button as an armature attached to
what screaming Vietnamese torturer in his brain?


October 18, 2009: a massacre of bright red leaves on fading
    autumn grass. Iran edging in.
                Persephone at large, whose icy winds
trim the branches as the current of the stream
    trims the trout.


Dreams at 78 are diced imagoes, static-fractured antiphons:
fume-like ghosts eel-intent on autumn's entropic arc.


Late Style: affirmation solely while facing annihilation.
What I know, I throw away.
What I have, I give away.


No antitheses. Reciprocal opposites.
Whatever I encounter here is another form of myself.


End-time dust blows through the Penney's on Monument Circle where
my mother worked after my father lost his job at Kingham Meatpacking.
I would visit her there occasionally. What a decent human being my
mother was, in spite of being so incapacitated, so at the mercy of her
Wabash background.

Having just driven up from Bloomington, I see her standing by the dress section, eager to greet me. I pass through the sleeves of my life, give her a little kiss. Why not a real kiss, a rain kiss? Why not a gorgeously-wrapped box with a baby Clayton Jr inside?

My mother    in the leg-irons of Indiana...


Listening to Betty Carter at Hotel Cro-Magnon,
I began to reconceive the Venus of Laussel:

It was her mouth, the under
altar, where oratory
made possible I heard
in her low notes the gain of black suffer
her moose spout, her jut
release, to involve Hades in mouth,
the range of her physical milking,
rugose, raisiny,
the deep sour sorb of her delta
gender become moot.
Emerging through the low notes:
a cave's stone wall,
fading painted animals,
the Paleolithic Muladhara Chakra
from which the fumes of sexual energy
suffused with imaginal energy coil—
vipers from a distance,
up close they have tender baby
snake faces,
sweet enough to nurse.


The alley I walked today—
I marveled at its lack of sturdy borders, admired its half-crushed cans,
house & auto rears, scuffed dirt & pebbles.
I walked a multi-level memory,

an everyday bigger than this alley-walked moment.
The day became an emerald I moved within, booted to the cosmos,
the air about me stiffer than my bones.
A redbud plunged my eyes back into eye-fisted midnight,
Pegasus enwebbed in a sea wall of moving clouds.
Between thumb & whorefinger, hooves flecked forth embers,
& I loved the slippage as I loved the traction, or the trenchancy,
     of my own abyssal loss.


Poetry is a melee; also a synthesis.
Midden phrases. Mind ladles down,
     as if through mineral declensions.


Everyday I offer self to the poem, & eat the poem as well.


The last written words of Mikhail Bakhtin:
"Nothing is absolutely dead; every meaning will celebrate its rebirth.
The problem of the great *temporality*."


Poetry should be everything that it can bear to be.


Be unbearable, poet—in every complexion of that word—
     staple a copula into the blowing hay.

                              January-October, 2013–June, 2016

Adrienne,   radiant horoscope of a completed circle,
death intervenes as the comedic plume.

Against your physical difficulties, you prevailed to write
a full blown & magisterial document of your life.

ADRIENNE RICH:
   lesbian coherence, and love.

"The institution of motherhood must be destroyed."

"*Self-trivialization, contempt for women, misplaced compassion, addiction;* if we
could purge ourselves of this quadruple poison, we would have minds
and bodies more poised for the act of survival and rebuilding."

"Art means nothing if it simply decorates the dinner table of power
which holds it hostage."

                    Wow, the morrow,
to mow through,       the majesty of lifting into view the grain.
                    Michelle
   your splendid partner.


            [Upon receiving the news from Michelle Cliff
               7:05 PM, 28 March 2012]

# SIDEWINDER

Lights disappear into the parking lot
before Tricho Salon. A gander is feeding in bushes below the plate glass.
It is drizzling. I sit here waiting for Caryl to have a pedicure,
still awed by the miracle of discovering Bud Powell in 1952 Indianapolis,
& Vallejo on a seppuku platform in 1963 Kyoto—
titbits of the perspiration of paradise, its spagyric dew.
Under the holy-dreadful lich gate of my mouth is
the lightning of my father's switch
            cut, as it were, from Hart Crane's behind.


Glintings of the sword play under Gemini,
lunge & parry, sidewinder through the self,
one's massive, corroded, serpentine, Babel-looted self.
Step into this florescent hive of mystery's gyre
where rebellion is contoured with ripped compassion.
Om of the dyadic foil looping through paradise unveiling
        whirlpools of multiple axes
rhizomic to their metaphoric dreamstock
where mirrors micturate mirrors &
the phantom of poetry speaks through Anna Akhmatova:


"The miraculous comes so close to the ruined, dirty houses,
something not known to anyone at all
but wild in our breast for centuries." And:


"Night of stone," yes, "whose bright enormous star
stares me straight in the eyes"


That star was the primordial Medusa,
stone the Upper Paleolithic cave walls lit solely by hand lamps,
Medusa whose ferocious, subtle, omen-perforated, & magical blindness
Cro-Magnon transformed into imagination.

The Greek Medusa subordinates animal parts to a basically human head.
The dots on her forehead may indicate the lion's superciliary
   tufts of hair above the eyes.
Imagine the snakes encircling the face as the winding corridors of a cave,
& the tusks or fangs as the ghosts of those dreadful encounters
where in total blackness, far from the cave entrance,
a human met a lion or a large cave bear.

Wild in our breasts, yes, but even more tempestuous in our minds:
the bending of the mind about animal staves
to create a cask for appetitional elixir.

Snake-wreathed slaughter face embedded in the wall.

In the Paleo-Pegasean gate of art there is to this night a carnivore mouth.

# A NEW UMBILICUS

A tangle of dream thoughts
that could not be unraveled
reveals
the dream's convexcavatious navel.

A new umbilicus into
Cro-Magnon's Neanderthal burial stare,

    the phantom of poetry
    uncoiling from its historic vessel
    nourished by
    this archaic placenta:

abyss forum between anus & sex
where the soul snake broods

(Artaud feared that God would murder him there—
interesting! That for Artaud God
might be most active on the balance pan between
shit & sperm, killing at fulcrum
anyone seeking to be fully born)

Shock holed Antonin in cross pull to himself,
mage of this abyss, as old as Dionysus
but not as old as Lascaux's bird-headed man
who IS
before culture fenced off with nature.

Hybrid release of his bird-headed mace
as bison paradise is penetrated.

And what is paradise—now? Add "now"
& you've leaned a rocket launcher against the word.
    *paired eyes*   *pariah dice*   *parrot ice*

Isis bursts of star ants, particles of an All
pregnant with the twin one must be to oneself.

Churn of translational axes,
fractured branching of the rhizomic dream
spread Cubistically across the night
emitting imaginal shoots:

fog veiling alders in goddess raiment
smashed crucible in which the serpents of the sun once basked
sin-trillion weight of gargoyles exhaling priest gas
Pandora's hexagram rampant with mangers
dumb numb uncaring death skinning me alive with beauty

"Only fury knowing its ground has staying power."


[In Memory of Adrienne Rich]

# THE DREAM'S NAVEL  *

For Stuart Kendall

Gotham Bar & Grill in Manhattan, dining with Caryl, Cecilia & Jim.
At a table near ours, alone, a woman in whose face I saw Death.
At one point she turned her head toward us:
I could only stay in her *black ray lane* a few seconds.

So, here we are. Sipping cheek timber, under the cistern eyes of earth's
granite-gated vineyard.

Cecilia Vicuña:   the shadow
                  is from the animal
                  you used to be
                  the shadow
                  is from  the one
                  you will be
                  the shadow is not from you
                  from them
                  from the one who passes
                  its not a shadow at all
                  it is the sound
                  of a shadow
                  it is the shadow
                  of the sound"

Freud: "There is a tangle of dream thoughts that cannot be unraveled.
This is the dream's navel, the spot where it reaches down into the
unknown."

Or as rephrased by Freud: "There is at least one spot in every dream at
which it is unplumbable—a navel as it were, that is its point of contact
with the unknown."

Freud also identifies the dream navel as a knot entangled with threads (evoking the Medusa's head of serpent hair covering the mother's "dangerous genitals"). He writes that some "dream thoughts are infinitely branching, rather than tangled…"

At one point he identifies the dream navel with the defile, or central neck, of a clepsydra, "where all forms resemble each other, where everything is possible."

The spot where this navel "reaches down into the unknown," can be envisioned as an Upper Paleolithic opening leading to a cave, the maternal interior being replaced by a limestone one; the "infinitely branching thoughts" becoming the engraved meanders on Rouffignac's "Red Ceiling with Serpentines," a surface covered with serpent-shaped signs.

Or as in Combarelle's Inner Gallery, the engraved creatures that only vaguely resemble anything that lived: animal-snouted archaic on the leash of,
>           or the harness of, a proto-alchemical mush,
>           sled beasts bounding in slow motion,
>           grotesque heads dissolving in grotto drift…

Can these silex-cut wall meanders and lines or black manganese finger strokes, unreadable but engageable, indicate a possible response of Cro-Magnon people in cave darkness to a dream's branchings & its grotesque inhabitants? Can we cut through time here and descend, without historical interference, through the palimpsestic layers of unconscious levels, to uncover the possible ignition of image making, in which non-human souls began to mingle with human souls?

"In fact," Gaston Bachelard proposes, "a need to animalize is at the origins of the imagination… its first function is to create animal forms."

Henri Michaux's stroke chaos, in which creature forms are evoked by tangled and knotted lines reminds us of the Cro-Magnon "creatures" verging on resembling yet undefined... As if we are in the presence of "nothing" in the process of "athing"...

Vicuña again: "The void, the forgotten aspect of each sound that is propelling us as we search for memory and oblivion at once..."

Soon I will be between here & there,
in the nowhere that is part of everywhere.
How will it not be to be nowhere?
Absence, Kenneth Grant writes, is the ever-present ultimate grounds.
To think into this most dense Un
as if I were to fall asleep & the universe were to vanish.
But to put it that way is ego grief
for when I am gone nothing will not have changed—
only the feelings of the few who are affected by my absence.
My absence...   As if absence were mine...

Old Whitman: "Have you learn'd lessons only of those who admired you, and were tender with you, and stood aside for you? Have you not learn'd great lessons from those who reject you, and brace themselves against you? Or who treat you with contempt, or dispute the passage with you?"

Willliam & Cid,
with you I've lived.
Corman said no
& Blake said yes.

We are free only to the degree that we are able to acknowledge the headless oarsmen rowing the heart skiff through the rainbow of a totality ebbing & flowing over
the rocks of man's now quite clearly unregenerate nature.

We have lost the *temenos,* the imaginative precinct
   in which a van Eyck, say,
could orchestrate a specific world

Dearth of polar bears. Dearth of honeybees.

   It is crying outside.

   *


   Image is the athanor in which I linguistize soul,
a dream umbilicus coiling down into the miracle of
Neanderthal tombstone cupules, Cro-Magnon engravings,
   earliest shamanic hybrids,
      through which a mistress spirit might rise,
electric with Tantrik lesions, from that serpent lounge
where the soul snake slumbers
until charmed up into a brain / body imaginarium.

My mind at base is a spermal animalcule
impregnated with female blood.
The Muladhara Chakra is not gendered.
   Neither is my imagination.
I reject duality & propose an orgy of contesting mind.
The soul was in exile even at Chauvet.

Proto-shamanism seems to have involved a visionary exchange
between Cro-Magnon & certain bison.
Paradise is a form of polymorphous merger
charged by the bathysphere of the poem
rising from engrailings where even squirrels reflect,
& robins ruminate: the animal lager…

   Bottom is crossed by
something alive, a crab or turtle brought up mud
regurgitated into a Cro-Magnon hand.

Ochre or manganese, discovered in descent
& mixed with cave water, palm pressed to stone
(a stone that in history becomes the omphalos, or om phallus),
released, leaving a "hand" without a hand,
negation's—or was it absence's?—first
                    imaginal presence.


The poem is from the beginning antiphonal,
hybridizing ancestral fauna in language-twisted straits.
Oh the difficulty of the soul! "You could not find the ends of the soul
though you traveled every way, so deep is its logos."
To Heraclitus, James Hillman responds: "the logos of the soul,
*Psychology,* implies the act of traveling the soul's labyrinth
in which *we can never go deep enough.*"
William Blake, naked, reading Genesis to naked Catherine
in their London "Arbor of Eden."


Jardin botanique, Bordeaux, 2008.
The bud & spoor density of a mauve Baudelairian incubation.
Tender vines erupting into fanged blooms...
Minute nomadic ants percolate the many-breasted
    Venus of the Plants.
Centuries pass... And the ghost of Henri Rousseau
        glides,   a virgin on a lost ark,
          in chime with cloned obsequies,
                fertile diapasons...


Fused to his centrovertic grappling,
into the aethercore the poet pours his siliceous soul.

# AN INTERVIEW WITH CLAYTON ESHLEMAN

**Stuart Kendall:** *From the very beginning of your career, or even from the beginning of your interest in poetry, you have been deeply engaged with translation and editing alongside your own writing. As a translator you've worked extensively with Spanish, French, Hungarian, and, to a lesser extent, Chinese language poetries. Your editorial work has been even more wide ranging. At the same time, your writing is deeply American, deeply concerned with your formation as a North American white male, and deeply concerned with the United States as a political entity, however flawed. In light of this, I'm wondering whether you might consider yourself a kind of transnational poet or, put differently and considering translation and editing is a kind of border-crossing gesture, whether you think this kind of border crossing is important for poets or poetry, either individually or collectively, outside of your own personal practice.*

**Clayton Eshleman:** To your language list, I would add Czech, as I worked with Frantisek Galan for some six months on Vladimir Holan's 31-page masterpiece, "A Night with Hamlet." We ended up with a few dozen problems we could not solve, so Michael Heim and I flew out to Austin TX where Frantisek lived in 1984 for a week and the three of us went through the poem word by word. Our final version with a note on Holan is in the 2005 edition of *Conductors of the Pit.*

Back in 1987, I entitled my first collection of prose writings *Antiphonal Swing,* based on the last line of Hart Crane's "The Bridge:" "whispers antiphonal in azure swing." At that time, I identified the "swing" as being between the erotic and the artistic, as well as between prose and poetry. I also drew upon the word "anatomy" (after Northrop Frye's referring to Blake's "The Marriage of Heaven and Hell" as an "anatomy"). Frye wrote that Blake's poem was less a dissection than a composite work that included as its "members" many of the forms and strategies of the art of writing. I think, then, that my "transnationality" as you put it, or "border-crossing," in an attempt to avoid the conventional pieties that inform so much of contemporary American poetry, involves a number of strategies: civil obligation (I prefer "civil" to "political), ekphrastic explorations, probings of the feminine as source and power (Barbara Walker's *A Woman's Encyclopedia of Myths and Secrets* was a wonderful fount of information in this regard), and my twenty-five year investigation of what I came to call "Upper Paleolithic Imagination & the Construction of the Underworld." As I wrote in the Introduction to *Juniper Fuse,* "To follow poetry back to Cro-Magnon metaphors not only hits real bedrock—a genuine back wall—but gains a connection to the continuum during which imagination first flourished."

In regards to civil obligations: given what the American government has been doing throughout the world from the end of World War II on, the American mind, into which news spatters daily, is now, more than ever, a roily swamp, at once chaotic and irrationally organized. The fate of American Indians and African-Americans is entangled with this complex. There is a whole new poetry to be written by Americans that pits our present-day national and international situation against these poisoned historical cores.

**SK:** *Is it too much to say that there is a double movement here: a movement away from those forces of restriction and disarticulation — the conventional pieties, the predictable and the aesthetically acceptable — and simultaneously a movement toward something else? I'm reminded of your take on Charles Olson's "istorin, to find out for oneself" where you "put the stress on 'out' or exit for the self," in the introduction to* Juniper Fuse. *As well as your remarks on Olson and Antonin Artaud in the first chapter of* Novices: A Study of Poetic Apprenticeship, *where your point is that the poet is always "stuffed as well as empty," stuffed with stories and figures, "all the initiations and stories of imaginative art," as you put it, but also empty, unformed, in Olson's term "zero." On the one hand the poet's project, as you describe it, is self-consciously critical – an act of disobedience – and on the other its goal is the emancipation of the self. How do you balance these tendencies, if in fact they are in competition with one another?*

**CE:** The dichotomy that you appear to be addressing can also be proposed as ego vs self. I think of the ego as the chauffeur of the self, the conscious mind vs the subconscious (possibly activated in the process of artistic creation) and the unconscious, which most of us only experience, and then usually in a confused way, in dreams. Northrop Frye has written, around 1990, that "What is needed for creation is a new bicameral mind in which something else supplants consciousness." I am not sure what he had in mind as this "something else" but it must involve some form of visionary activity, which could include hallucination, and might be a way of dreaming awake, or a mingling of the unconscious and the subconscious minds. There are aspects of the poetry of Antonin Artaud, Aimé Césaire, and Robert Kelly, for example, that engage what I think Frye has in mind here.

My *Novice* comments concerning the poet being "stuffed but empty" probably are more relevant when applied to apprenticeship than to the work of mature poets. "Stuffed" at least in my case was the situation I found myself in while living in Kyoto in the early 1960s when the full weight of what seemed to be involved in becoming poet swept over me. I was "stuffed" with the unexamined first 27 years of my life, and facing for the first time the sexism, prejudice, rule following and acting out of what Indianapolis had proposed that I was. The weight of all of this sealed me up when I tried to write poetry. Thus "stuffed" got reprogramed as "empty," or blocked. In desperation, my being cried out for a vision, or some indication that my poetic apprenticeship (which I had decided by early 1962 was to be a translation of Vallejo's *Poemas humanos*) meant anything at all.

As some readers will know, I had a vision at this time: that autumn I was in the habit of reading in the backyard of our Kyoto residence by the web of a large red, green and yellow garden spider. After one stormy night, I went to the persimmon tree with the web to find it torn, and the spider gone. I had a very peculiar reaction to this "loss": for several days I felt nauseous and absurd. A week later, after having tea with Joanne Kyger north of Kyoto where she lived with Gary Snyder, I got on my motorcycle and headed back into the city. As I described in *Novices* (in greater detail than I will do here), I suddenly began to hallucinate and, terrified that I would have an accident, pulled into the parking lot for Nijo Castle tourist buses, got off the motorcycle and began to circumambulate the castle. At the northwest corner I felt commanded to look up, which I did to see, some 30 feet above my head, the spider which was now life-sized and completely red flexing in her web. After maybe a half minute the vision began to fade. The next day I realized that I had been given a totemic gift that would direct my relation to poetry.

As I continued to struggle to get Vallejo's complex and complicated Spanish into English, I increasingly had the feeling that I was struggling more with a man than with a text and that the struggle was a matter of my becoming or failing to become a poet.

During this period I translated every afternoon in a downtown Kyoto coffee shop called Yorunomado (= Night Window). In "The Duende" section of "The Book of Yorunomado" (the only poem I completed to any real satisfaction while living in Japan), I envisioned myself as a kind of angelless Jacob wrestling with a figure who possessed a language the meaning of which I was attempting to wrest away. I lose the struggle and find myself on a seppuku platform in medieval Japan, being commanded by Vallejo (now playing the role of an overlord) to disembowel myself. I do so, cutting the ties to my "given life" and releasing a daemon named Yorunomado who, until that point (my vision told me) had been chained to an altar in my solar plexus. Thus at this point the fruits of my struggle with Vallejo were not a successful literary translation but an imaginative advance in which a third figure emerged from my intercourse with the text. Thus death and regeneration = seppuku and the birth of Yorunomado, or a breakthrough into what might be called sacramental existence. Years later, I noted Hans Peter Duerr writing in *Dreamtime:* "Only a person who had seen his 'animal part'; who had 'died', could consciously live in culture."

In "Self As Selva," a poem from a new manuscript called "Penetralia," I write: "Self as engine as well as brimming circumference. Self as one's mind after & *before birth:* differentiated identity & the undifferentiated lower levels where specters from humanity's past still dwell.... Self as selva, a liana matrix of twin-twisted lingo."

**SK:** *Shifting the movement I proposed into a psychological topography is helpful, I think, in drawing it into conversation with a wider range of ideas. Partly here I'm interested in the extent to which a poet's work might remain confined to a self-conscious criticality, positively or negatively, without descending into the undifferentiated lower levels of the self, or conversely, a poet's work might be entirely devoted to such a descent, without situating that descent in relation to a social reality. I'm interested in the mechanisms by which you remain committed and keep yourself committed to or attentive to both of these realms. This is, I think, ultimately a question about your creative practice. In the example you've just mentioned, your engagement with Vallejo's work as a translator, alongside your poetic attempts to write your way out of Indiana, seems to have provoked a visionary experience, which itself became foundational in your ongoing work. I don't want to reduce this complex moment and experience to* *some kind of formula for poetry, but I'm wondering to what extent this kind of prim-ing is necessary for sustaining a creative life in poetry. I'd also like to hear more about what you mean by the phrase "sacramental existence"?*

**CE:** I find your first question, asking the extent to which a poet might con-fine his work to self-conscious criticality without engaging the self, impos-sible to answer. "The extent to which" is the rub, and without a particular poet (or dimension of my own work) to look at, I don't know how to take on your question. If you have a poet you feel is an example of this situation, I will try to respond, assuming I am familiar with the work. You then won-der about the mechanisms by which I engage both realms. I draw a blank with the word "mechanisms." Finally you ask another "to what extent" ques-tion regarding my spider vision followed by my self-destruction and the birthing of Yorunomado. As I think I wrote, these two events are founda-tional to what I have been able to accomplish as a poet over the decades. Invented mythical figures like Yorunomado and Niemonjima that are em-broiled in the action in my book *Coils* (1973) complexed some of the au-tobiographical consternation in that book.

The crucial event in my development after leaving Japan in 1964 was my 1974 discovery of Cro-Magnon cave art in southwestern France. Sud-denly, in the spring of 1974 I was completely caught up in the deep past and what possibly was the origin of art as we know it today. This grand transpersonal realm (without a remaining history or language) was about as far away from my Indianapolis adolescence as could be, and as I re-searched and revisited the painted caves throughout the late 1970s, 1980s, and 1990s, this focus released me from my preoccupations with my back-ground as well as my working with Blakean mythic strategies. In many ways, *Juniper Fuse* is the key book of my career.

By "sacramental existence" I mean to suggest that the birth of Yoruno-mado enabled me to escape from the tyranny of time into a "spontaneous" creation of myth making. For an instant I was the master of my own death and regeneration and released from the stuffed/empty impasse of the In-diana background. I was in touch with one of the essential functions of myth: the re-entry into Great Time, or sacred Time.

**SK:** *I take your point about the phrase "to what extent." I'm tiptoeing around a problem in poetry and poetic vocation. I think it's fair to say that not all poets have a visionary experience of initiation into or confirmation of poetic vocation. In an interview published a few years ago in* The Wolf, *you remarked: "nearly all of the poetry reviewed, lauded, and prized today, is not the real thing." Is visionary experience or confirmation required for poetry to be real poetry, as you understand it? Beyond that, could you say a little bit more about the relationship between the foundation of your work in your visionary experiences in Japan and the ways that your research into the painted caves built upon or extended that foundation?*

**CE:** My comments that you quote from *The Wolf* interview refer mainly to the extent to which "creative writing" (child of the university degree writing programs) is replacing poetry. Of course there is no ultimate criteria for what makes a poet engaging, but my experience has been that with a few marvelous exceptions like Rimbaud or Lautréamont it involves a self-taught apprenticeship based on a study of a few chosen masters in American poetry and hopefully a few masters in international poetries. My fantasy is that the young writer would learn more crouched by the banks of the Amazon with a knapsack full of books than he would in creative writing workshops.

The kind of experiences I had in Kyoto in the early 60s are not a requirement for someone becoming a poet. They were a product of my own background and fix, and everyone has a unique situation in this regard. I think you know that my range of interest in contemporary poetry is wide and varied. I published Charles Simic and Jorie Graham in *Sulfur* magazine as well as Charles Bernstein and Rachel Blau DuPlessis. I suppose a careful reader could find links between the poetries of the poets I have translated, but poets such as Vladimir Holan, Bei Dao, César Vallejo and Antonin Artaud represent as many differences as things in common.

My crucial perception concerning the origin and elaboration of Upper Paleolithic cave imagery is carefully set forth on p. xvi in *Juniper Fuse*. Briefly, it concerns my intuition (underscored by my reading of James Hillman's *The Dream and the Underworld*) that such images were motivated by a crisis in which Cro-Magnon people began to separate the animal out of their about-to-be human heads and to project it onto cave walls (as well as onto a variety of portable tools and weapons made out of the animals themselves).

There is a ten-year interval between my initial Yorunomado transformation and my perception concerning the separating out of the animal as a formative function of Cro-Magnon imagination. In both of these cases, separated by thousands of years of culture dynamics, a mysterious intuitive projection involved the need to transform one's present situation into a larger, more mind-engaging possibility. I transformed a Kyoto coffee-shop into an imaginal daemon; in the Cro-Magnon situation (which goes back as far as 32,000 years), and in a way that can be considered proto-shamanic (another link), a blank cave wall, under minimal lighting, became a kind of dancing ground for a hand gripping a piece of charcoal.

**SK:** *I love your fantasy of a poet on the banks of the Amazon with a backpack full of books. You've also mentioned the reading and research that guided and informed your writing on the painted caves in particular. I also know that you read other types of research materials when working on your translations. How does research feed your work? Is it essential to it or supplemental to it?*

**CE:** As the first poet to do what Charles Olson referred to as "a saturation job" on Upper Paleolithic cave art, I was really starting from scratch, I had to make myself responsible for much of what archeologists had written about them as well as to study other thinkers who might help me support my own evolving point of view. Thus I not only read the work of the Abbés Breuil and Glory, Annette Laming, André and Arlette Leroi-Gourhan, S. Giedion, Max Raphael, Paolo Graziosi, Alexander Marshack, Jean Clottes, Margaret W. Conkey, and Paul Bahn, I also read C.G. Jung, Sandor Ferenczi, Géza Róheim, Mikhail Bakhtin, Weston La Barre, Charles Olson, N.O. Brown, Kenneth Grant, James Hillman, Hans Peter Duerr, Barbara MacLeod, and Maxine Sheets-Johnstone. I also sought to match my pluralistic approach with varying styles. *Juniper Fuse* is of poetry, prose poetry, essays, lectures, notes, dreams and visual reproductions.

Translation, research-wise, was a different matter. The two years that I lived in Kyoto (1962–1964) I visited the poet, editor, and translator, Cid Corman, at The Muse Coffee Shop, in downtown Kyoto, in the evening once a week. Corman was then editing the third series of his magazine *origin,* and he already had an impressive track record as a translator of Catullus, Rimbaud, Basho, Rilke, Ungaretti, Char, Montale, Daumal, Daive,

Ponge, Celan, and Artaud. Corman is one of the great poetry translators of our time. Before talking at The Muse with Cid about translation, I thought the goal was to take a literal draft and *interpret* everything that was not acceptable English. By interpret I mean: to monkey with words, phrases, punctuation, line breaks, even stanza breaks, turning the literal into something that was not an original poem in English but—and here is the rub—something that because of the liberties taken was also not faithful to the original itself. Ben Belitt's Neruda versions or Robert Lowell's *Imitations* come to mind as interpretative translations. Corman taught me to respect the original at every point, to check everything (including words I thought I knew), to research arcane and archaic words, and to invent English words for coined words—in other words, to aim for a translation that was absolutely accurate *and* up to the performance level of the original. Corman's translation information was so valuable that I have never felt a need to seek out translation theories.

I began to translate Vallejo while a student at Indiana University in the late 1950s and completed *The Complete Poetry of César Vallejo* (University of California Press, 2007), some 45 years later. During this nearly life-long saga, given the difficulties in rendering Vallejo accurately, certain co-translators were invaluable in my work: I owe an enormous gratitude to Maureen Ahern, Américo Ferrari, José Rubia Barcia, Efrain Kristal, and José Cerna-Bazan.

The current collection of my *Essential Poetry* includes 223 poems from over 1000 published poems from this 50 year period. There are 70 pages of notes following the poems and reading these notes will give the reader a sense of the research I have done in writing some of my own poems. In particular I would like to point out the 4 pages of notes, based on Weston La Barre's *Muelos; A Stone Age Superstition about Sexuality,* for the poem "Navel of the Moon," and the 4 pages of notes, based on Sandor Ferenczi's *Thalassa: A Theory of Genitality,* for the poem "Thalassa Variations." James Hillman's writings have been especially valuable for my poetry. In *A Sulfur Anthology,* based on the magazine I founded and edited from 1981 to 2000, to be published in fall 2015 by Wesleyan University Press, the reader will find my interview discussion with Hillman on psychology and poetry.

**SK:** *In your "triadic dialogue with Paul Hoover and Maxine Chernoff" published in* The Price of Experience, *you remark that, "working on poems is mainly working on self, the subconscious as warp, consciousness as woof, while keeping self positioned in the actual world." How is your research related to this notion of poetry as work on the self?*

**CE:** Good question. Here is one example of the way my research can relate to writing poems that relate to the self.

Over the years I have pondered Sandor Ferenczi's *Thalassa: A Theory of Genitality,* and wondered how his unique argument might shed light on the origin of image-making. In brief, Ferenczi proposes that the whole of life is determined by a tendency to return to the womb. Equating the process of birth with the transition of animal life from water to land, he links coitus to what he calls "thalassal regression": "the longing for sea-life from which man emerged in primeval times." He explains what he means by an "attempt to return to the mother's womb"—and thus to the oceanic womb of life itself—in the following way:

> If we now survey the evolution of sexuality from the thumb-sucking of the infant through the self-love of genital onanism to the heterosexual act of coitus, and keep in mind the complicated identifications of the ego with the penis and with the sexual secretion, we arrive at the conclusion that the purpose of this whole evolution, therefore the purpose likewise of the sex act, can be none other than an attempt at the beginning clumsy and fumbling, then more consciously purposive, and finally in part successful—to return to the mother's womb, where there is no painful disharmony between ego and environment as characterize existence in the external world. The sex act achieves this transitory regression in a three-fold manner: the whole organism attains the goal by purely hallucinatory means, somewhat as in sleep; the penis, with which the organism as a whole has identified itself, attains it partially or symbolically, while only the sexual secretion

possesses the prerogative, as representative of the ego and
its narcissistic double, the genital, of attaining in reality
to the womb of the mother.

In one respect, "Thalassa Variations" is a compression of, and variation
on, Ferenczi's argument.

To my knowledge, N.O. Brown is the only writer to have heretofore
assimilated Ferenczi's theory of genitality into a larger dimension including
creativity. In *Love's Body,* Brown even acknowledges the Upper Paleolithic
caves as the places in which history begins. Like Ferenczi, Brown is a
Freudian, and while he views the Upper Paleolithic caves as the first
labyrinths, he fails to reflect on what seems to be their most distinctive
characteristic: they were not merely wandering places, or even dancing
enclosures, but the sites for some of the earliest image-making. Following
Ferenczi, Brown views genitality as ultimately ungratifying, in effect a trap.
Ferenczi's proposal that we desire to return to the womb and obviously
cannot, in Brown's terms, becomes the limitation he calls "genital organi-
zation."

Since Brown also draws upon William Blake's vision of four mental states
potentially operative in humanity, it may be useful to point out that from a
Blakean viewpoint, to be confined to "genital organization" is to be arrested
at the third level of mental expansion (see the poem, "The Crystal Cabinet"),
or to be in the State of Beulah. In other words, Blake appears to mean that
those who settle for sexual gratification alone are not fully, in his terms,
"human." For Blake, there is a fourth state, the State of Eden, in which imag-
ination is engaged *and* realized, and in which art that we might call great is
created. Blake's image for this state is fire in love with fire (from which Yeats
undoubtedly got his image of creative unity: the dancer as unidentifiable
apart from the dance). While there may be a temporary "gratification of de-
sire" between two people in the State of Beulah, in the State of Eden the
other vanishes, and for the individual to avoid plunging into the lowest
State—the State of Ulro, in which one is simply unimaginatively stuck with
oneself—one must practice a sort of imaginative androgyny called art.
While Brown does not include cave art in his discussion of the labyrinth, he
does view coitus as a fallen metaphor for poetry.

Were Blake alive today, I am confident that he would make the connection I am about to make: the womb that cannot be returned to à la Ferenczi was imaginatively re-entered when Cro-Magnon crawled into a cave and drew, painted or sculpted an image. I conjecture that one impulse for going into the cave was orgasm itself, which flooded the mind with fantasy material that sought a fulfillment beyond survival concerns. Image-making, then, can be seen as the attempt to unblock the paradoxical male impasse of genital expression, or, in my poem, it is what the belling deer image "says" to its Cro-Magnon maker on his back in that cul-de-sac in Le Portel: "Image is / the imprint of uncontainable omega, / life's twin." In the same stanza, I attempted to draw upon the Freudian/Ferenczian theory of the sexual stages of development, working with the possibility that from childhood on, oral, anal, and genital formations are incorporated in image-making, which for the creative individual becomes a kind of fourth dimension (or State à la Blake) that includes the earlier three *and* pushes beyond.

**SK:** *Great example. The poem in this case is a variation on motifs and ideas drawn from Ferenczi, Brown, and Blake, in dialogue with images from Le Portel as well as your personal - in fact intimate — life with Caryl. It's psychoanalysis, poetry, the Paleolithic record, and personal experience fused together. I also recall that the word variation carries musical reference for you as well: from the impact of your discovery of variations on melody in jazz music. And then too I know that "Thalassa Variations" is a kind of variation on a theme you explored in a previous poem, "This I Call Holding You"(published in* What She Means *(1978)). Can you talk about the persistence of themes or topics in your work? Is there a difference for you between a recurrent theme and a re-written one?*

**CE:** In a poem called "The Tjurunga" (*Anticline*, p, 17; see the Note on pp. 75–76 for the meaning of this word), I propose a kind of complex mobile made up of the authors, mythological figures and acts, whose shifting combinations undermined and reoriented my life during my poetic apprenticeship in Kyoto in the early 1960s. At a remove now of some 50 years I also see these forces as a kind of GPS constantly "recalculating" as they closed and opened door after door. Making up the mobile in this poem were: *Coatlicue* (the Aztec idol with the sacrificed woman Coatlicue inside her), sub-incision (the primeval rite conferring androgynity upon its male participant), Bud Powell, César Vallejo, and the bird-headed man (from the Shaft in Lascaux). After this list of powers, I wrote:

> These nouns are also nodes in a constellation called
> Clayton's Tjurunga. The struts are threads
> in a web. There is a life blood flowing through
> these threads. Coatlicue flows into Bud Powell,
> César Vallejo into sub-incision. The bird-headed man
> floats right below
> > > the pregnant spider
> > centered in the Tjurunga

When I was 16 years old, I taped two quarters to an order form in *Downbeat* magazine and mailed it off for a 45 RPM recording with Lennie Tristano's "I Surrender Dear" on one side, Bud Powell's "Tea for Two" on the other. I listened to the Powell piece again and again trying to grasp the difference between the song line and what Powell was doing to and with it. Somehow an idea vaguely made its way through: you don't have to play somebody else's melody—you can improvise (how?), make up your own tune! WOW—really? You mean I don't have to repeat my parents? I don't have to "play their melody" for the rest of my life?

You ask if there is, for me, a difference between a recurrent theme and a re-written one. There is, but both are operative in my body of work: early inspirational figures such as Powell, Hart Crane, and Chaim Soutine return in poems from time to time (there are three pieces on Powell, six on Crane, and six on Soutine). As they do so, they are recast into current pre-occupations and challenges. Crane's metaphoric shifts evoke improvisational moves in bebop or strokes in a de Kooning painting of the 1960s. Reading Crane is like watching colored fragments in a turned kaleidoscope slip into new symmetries, then rearrange again. "New thresholds, new anatomies!" indeed!

I saw my first Soutine in 1963 in the Ohara Museum of Art, Kurushiki, Japan, *Hanging Duck,* painted in Paris around 1925. Seeing this painting was so riveting that I recall nothing else in the museum. It was a hybrid fusion, at once a flayed man hung from a pulpy wrist and flailing, with gorgeous white wings attached to his leg stumps—and a gem-like putrescent bird, snagged by one leg, in an underworld filled with bird-beaked monsters and zooming gushes of blood color and sky-blue paint.

My life has been blessed with a number of dear painter friends including William Paden, Leon Golub, and Nora Jaffe. Over the decades I have written pieces about all of them, and with Paden (*Brother Stones,* 1968) and Jaffe (*Realignment,* 1974) I co-authored books. Over a period of some 35 years I composed seven poems, reviews and essays on the paintings of Leon Golub. The most ambitious piece is a poem called "Monumental," which I assembled for Leon's public memorial program at the Cooper Union's Great Hall in NYC, 2005.

Including the pieces based on Ice Age cave art, I have written over 150 poems on art and artists. In a 2005 statement for *deep THERMAL,* a book I co-authored with the painter Mary Heebner, I wrote: "I am interested in what I see in paintings as well as what the paintings see in me. I found in certain Mary Heebner watercolors a resonating psychic stimulation and attempted to improvise on the words, narrative nodes and associational "chains" they flushed forth." For many years, the following words of Baudelaire, from "the Salon of 1846," have inspired such workings: "I sincerely believe that the best criticism is that which is both amusing and poetic: not a cold, mathematical criticism which, on the pretext of explaining everything, has neither love nor hate, and voluntarily strips itself of every shred of temperament. But, seeing that a fine picture is nature reflected by an artist, the criticism which I approve will be that picture reflected by an intelligent and sensitive mind. Thus the best account of a picture may well be a sonnet or an elegy."

At the base of these recurrent workings on and with musicians and painters are some thoughts elaborated in a 2009 poem "Inner Parliaments" (published in *Anticline*):

I
is an arm with a hand.
How did I first announce self?
In the Upper Paleolithic, it placed its hand on a cave wall,
spat red ochre around the hand, withdrew the hand,

leaving an I-negative on the wall.
Is what we now call art an elaboration of this I-negative,
Kafka's "What is laid upon us to accomplish is the negative,
the positive is already given"?

**SK:** *Considering this, another phrase of yours springs to mind:"the name encanyoned river."Your body of work reads as an extended and shifting kaleidoscope of dialogues, considerations, encounters, and engagements with words, ideas, images, places, objects and experiences. Aside from the remark from Baudelaire that you mention, are there other poets or writers whose ekphrastic writing particularly inspired your ongoing engagement with the visual arts? I suppose I'm thinking in particular of Artaud and Henri Michaux as two poets whose poetry has been meaningful to you and who also wrote compellingly about the visual arts.*

**CE:** My earliest recollections of involvement with the visual arts goes back to reading the "funnies" in daily Indianapolis newspapers, collecting comic books, and drawing my own cartoon strips. When I was around ten years old, my mother offered an art student from John Herron School of Art in Indianapolis a free dinner and a couple of dollars to give me and my pal Jack Wilson weekly cartoon lessons. I vaguely recall one of my cartoons winning a prize at some contest in a downtown department store. In my junior and senior years at Shortridge High School I took some figure drawing classes and did quite well in them. I sketched a drawing of a hobo who had been paid to pose that my mother put up on our living room wall for many years. I think I might have become a painter had there been a more intense local art atmosphere to inspire me at the time.

My mother also arranged for me to take piano lessons from a neighborhood piano teacher when I was six years old and the lessons continued up through my teenage years when I studied with the concert pianist Ozan Marsh. I was playing Chopin's "Revolutionary Etude" on one hand, and on the other, starting to hang out at local blues and jazz clubs, such as The Surf Club on West 16th Street where one Saturday afternoon Wes Montgomery invited me to sit in with his band. In my last response to your queries, I cited my discovery of Bud Powell when I was sixteen, and a couple years later, in the summer of 1953, I rode out to Los Angeles with a friend and studied briefly with Bud's brother Richie, and Marty Paitch. A few years later, while studying Philosophy at Indiana University I discovered poetry moreorless on my own, and through my meeting Jack and Ruth Hirschman and Mary Ellen Solt was put in touch with the writings of the Beats and Black Mountain-associated poets, as well as many of the great 20th century European poets.

You ask if there were any particular poets who inspired my now lifelong involvement with ekphrastic writing. My earliest memory of writing a poem about a painting was an occasion in one of Sam Yellen's creative writing classes when he assigned us to compose a poem about a painting. I chose Picasso's *Guernica* and went ahead to write a second poem on Bosch's *The Garden of Earthly Delights.* The Bosch poem was published in *The College Art Journal,* one of my first publications. Earlier, I mentioned my discovery of Soutine in Japan in 1963, and I think it was his paintings that made me really want to engage paintings and artists in poetry. None of the poets I was reading in the 60s and 70s had a compelling ekphrastic focus, or if they did, I was not aware of it.

Michaux and Artaud: I have written two pieces on Michaux, and I will let my opening salvo at the beginning of "Michaux. 1956" (1956 was his big mescaline-oriented year) represent that connection:

> There is in Michaux an emergent face/non-face always in formation. Call it "face before birth." Call it our thingness making faces. Call it tree bole or toadstool spirits, *anima mundi* snout, awash in ephemerality, anti-anatomical, the mask of absence, watercolor by a blind child, half-disintegrated faces of souls in Hades pressing about the painter Ulysses-Michaux as, over his blood trench of ink, he converses with his hermaphroditic muse…

Artaud is an even more complex figure. I was introduced to him in 1965 in the Hirschman *Artaud Anthology* which Jack sent me when Barbara and I were living in Lima, Peru. Over the decades I have written nine pieces on Artaud, or out of, into, Artaud. For someone who has yet to meet Artaud, I highly recommend the four books, all in print, that the English essayist/novelist Stephen Barber has written on this writer. Antonin Artaud is one of the greatest examples in art of the imaginative retrieval of a life that was beyond repair. What he ultimately accomplished should bear a torch through the dark nights of all our souls. Given the new perspectives on his writings and drawings that he created in what may now be considered his second major period—from his regeneration in the Rodez asylum in 1945 to his death outside of Paris in 1948—I have focused on that second period in the translations that I have done of his poetry and prose: *Watch-fiends & Rack Screams,* unfortunately published by Exact Change Press in 1995 which has not paid me royalties for a number of years and refuses to release rights to my translation so that it can be republished with new translations in an even more ample presentation of Artaud's accomplishments during this late period.

**SK:** *Earlier in this conversation you observed that the most crucial event for your development as a poet after leaving Japan was your discovery of the Paleolithic painted caves. I don't want to argue with that observation.We've also just been talking about your wider engagement with the visual arts and music. I know that civic engagement is also important to you.When did you first become civically or politically aware and engaged?*

**CE:** I began to become politically aware in Lima, Peru, 1965. I was shocked by the extent of terrible poverty there and began to wander the *barriadas* (slum neighborhoods) in an attempt to really get what they were under my skin. In my book *Walks,* published in 1967, "Walk VI" focuses on one of these excursions. At the same time, I was working for the Peruvian North American Culture Institute, editing a new bilingual magazine I called *Quena* (after the one-holed Peruvian flute). I had gone to the Institute looking for work teaching English as a second language as my wife (who was quite pregnant) and I had no money when we arrived. We had gone to Lima because I wanted to inspect the worksheets for Vallejo's never-completed *Poemas humanos* which were in the Vallejo widow's possession there.

Anyway, I included in the first some 300 page first issue of the magazine, 5 poems by Javier Heraud (translated by Paul Blackburn) that he had written before going to Cuba several years earlier. Before that trip, Heraud was apolitical and the poems Paul translated were old-fashioned nature poems. However, while in Cuba, Heraud became politicized and when he returned to Peru in 1963 as a member of the Ejercito de Liberacion National, he was shot by local police while drifting in a dugout near Puerto Maldonado. His death as a would-be guerilla created a scandal in Lima and because the Institute, it turned out, was receiving funding from the USIS, the American Ambassador in Lima (who had been shown the *Quena* manuscript by my concerned boss at the Institute) said that the Heraud translations could not appear in a publication sponsored by the Institute. I refused to remove the Heraud poems and was fired.

While all of this was going on, I discovered that a number of Peruvian poets who I had become acquainted with thought I was an American spy because I was employed by the Institute. So I guess you could say that I was thrust into a new and complex political situation through going to Peru and through assembling this first issue of *Quena* with Heraud in it.

When Barbara, the recently-born Matthew, and I moved to NYC in 1966 I discovered that my old painter friends Leon Golub and Irving Petlin were directors of an ad hoc organization "Artists Against the War" and I quickly became in charge of the poets participating in demonstrations throughout the city.

**SK:** *Picking up the notion of a "constellation" from the passage you quoted a moment ago from your poem The Tjurunga, wherein the "nouns are also nodes in a constellation called / Clayton's Tjurunga." A constellation is distinct from a series or some other form of linear or logical arrangement. I see the notion as being related to your take on the "anatomy" in Blake via Northrop Frye. Are you self-conscious in your approach to assembling or arranging the constellation of materials at the level of the poem or at the level of a collection of poems? A piece like Notes from a Visit to Le Tuc D'Audoubert, for example, shifts registers in one way, while, on the other hand, Juniper Fuse, as a book, constellates elements in, it seems to me, a different way.*

**CE:** "Notes on a Visit to Le Tuc d'Audoubert" is an anatomy, in Northrop Frye's sense, in as much as it is, let us say, a structural make-up of a poetic organism with contrasting parts, such as poetry, prose poetry, paragraphs, and visual "punctuation." In my note on this poem in *Juniper Fuse,* I mention that years later I realized that these "Notes" were the nuclear form for a book that would become an amplification of its multiple genres. Included in this amplification would be photographs, drawings, extensive commentary, chronologies, and such invented daemons as Kashkaniraqmi, Atlementheneira, and Savolathersilonighcock, joining the earlier Yorunomado and Niemonjima.

*Juniper Fuse* is also a constellation, or an assemblage, that is loosely chronological with the earliest pieces written in 1978 and final sections composed in 2002. I say "loosely" because this chronological arrangement is not always followed. When I was working out the final Table of Contents I saw that certain pieces written in different periods belonged together so I broke up a strict chronological order to take that sense of the book into consideration.

All of my books, over the decades, are, in general, chronological, allowing the above-described exception various degrees of play.

While living in Kyoto (1962–1964) I spent a great deal of time breaking my head over Blake's "Prophetic Books." Titles such as "The Book of Yorunomado" are based on Blake having called his shorter Prophecies "Books," like "The Book of Ahania" and "The Book of Los." Gary Snyder writes somewhere that when he came unannounced to visit me one afternoon he found me asleep on the tatami in my workroom and left after deciding not to wake me up. I had actually passed out that day while reading Blake's "Book of Urizen."

These "books" that I was composing in Kyoto (and later in Bloomington, Indiana, in 1964–65), were sections of a Blake-inspired long poem to be called "The Tsuruginomiya Regeneration" (the title coming from the name of the Shinto shrine across the road from the Ibuki home where Barbara and I were living in 1963–64). I started this poem initially as a marriage celebration for Paul and Sara Blackburn but given the extent to which I was confused and lost finding my way in poetry (and attempting to translate Vallejo's *Poemas humanos*) the "Regeneration" quickly became a Blakean-nuanced quagmire. In the early 1970s I put several of the most coherent "Regeneration" "books" together with some recent poems to compose *Coils* (1973).

**SK:** *As a long-time reader of your work, I find the relationship between* The Tsuruginomiya Regeneration *and* Coils *a compelling conundrum. You've mentioned that you published a great deal of the* Regeneration *in journals and chapbooks. Was there something about attempting to bring the pieces together into a single* *collection that brought out aspects of the individual sections that you felt didn't work or what it something related to the collection as such? I guess I'm wondering about the difference between writing a successful poem and bringing poems together as a successful collection. In this context though, I also recall a remark of yours from an interview originally published in* Atropos, *later collected in* Antiphonal Swing, *wherein you said that you didn't like much of what you wrote between 1966 and 1970, citing a shift in your habits of editing and revising your work before during and after that period.*

**CE:** Each "Book" or section of "The Tsuruginomiya Regeneration" seemed to be the beginning of a new long poem. I was lost, and unable to discover an all-over plan I could write into. I was way too haunted by Blake's abandoned manuscript of "The Four Zoas" (originally called "Vala"), and my attempts to ingest his long poems (or "Prophecies") at that time was probably a mistake as their mythic turmoil mainly muddled my personal turmoil rather than suggesting a way that I might proceed in coming to terms with my poetic apprenticeship. Two of the "Books" that I kept as part of *Coils,* "The Book of Yorunomado," and "The Book of Niemonjima" have some very good writing in them with the Blakean influence helping me to go beyond what I would otherwise been able to write.

I never again attempted a long poem, or epic. I have done a few extended pieces, like "Tavern of the Scarlet Bagpipe" (42 pages), my imaginative investigation of the great and profoundly mysterious *Garden of Earthly Delights* by Hieronymus Bosch, "Anatomy of the Night" (56 pages), an anatomy of sorts, made up poetry, prose, and quoted passages from the work of Roheim, Reich, Hillman, Alvarez, Cioran, Djuna Barnes, and James Hamilton-Paterson, as well as some material from my own writing between 1983 and 2011, and "The Moistinsplendor" (48 pages), an LSD-inspired rant, about which I have written: "On one level the poem is a struggle to think against erasure. At the moment I would seem to focus on something, the drug kicked it into a kaleidoscopic maze. My experience with LSD was that it operated mentally like the amusement park ride called the loop-the-loop. I found myself constantly wildly swinging between what appeared to be an imaginative insight and having the insight pulled inside out and being slapped in the face with it. When a line suddenly looked peculiar or dumb I would immediately write down the next thing that came to mind. There was no revision. I had the feeling, as peculiar as it may sound, that by drinking wine while I wrote that I was grounding myself and keeping the LSD from whirling me into a lockjaw abyss."

As for the period between 1966 and 1970: including translations and chapbooks I published twelve books during this period. I think the best of my own work are probably *Walks, The House of Okumura, Indiana,* and *The House of Ibuki.* I have included 22 poems from these four collections in *The Essential Poetry 1960–2015* (Black Widow Press). That is not much, in my case, for four years of work, and it mainly shows that at that time I was often unable to edit my poems into precise, imaginative structures or, from a present point of view, to determine between a poem that worked and one that did not. The first book in which I hit the stride that I like to think I have maintained with increasing acuity ever since is the 1981 *Hades In Manganese.*

**SK:** *Some of your most recent poetry strikes me as among the strongest of your career. I'm particularly thinking of* An Anatomy of the Night *and* The Jointure, *among other recent pieces. And I'm thinking in particular of the fluidity with which you shift directions, depths, and registers in these writings, covering an enormous range of thought and human feeling. Despite the range of content, the writing is, I think, unmistakably yours not only because it represents your ongoing thought but also because of the way that the materials come together or perhaps rather intersect with or overlay and impact one another. The work seems to have inverted the figure you advanced a moment ago: if the early epic failed to come together for lack of a structure into which you could write, the current work seems to emerge from a core of concern that is all of a piece. All or nearly all of your more recent work seems to be part of an unfolding, expansive epic.*

*From reading other interviews and remarks you've made about your writing process, I know that your relationship to editing has changed over the course of your career. How large an impact has your editing process had on your work and on your recent work in particular?*

**CE:** Over the past few years it has become increasingly difficult for me to engage material for a possible poem and then to realize the evolution of this material in a way that I find satisfactory. Most of the 66 poems in my latest completed manuscript, "Penetralia" (to be published by Black Widow

Press in 2017) were completed between 2008 and 2015 and the last half-dozen, which include "The Jointure," required many drafts to realize. I think the 16-page "The Jointure" must have close to 150 worksheets.

Such difficulties lead me to the following considerations: In my 40s, 50s, and 60s, I often found myself in a contrapuntal relationship to what occurred in writing: I would begin a poem with an idea of an impulse to engage particular material and the writing proceeded via thematic perceptions as well as spontaneous dream-like input which thematic material appeared to flush out. Such was not like dreaming awake. Rather, it was as if my intentions in a poem beckoned to my subconscious which like a helpful handmaiden offered to contribute material that sometimes contradicted, sometimes improvised, upon what my conscious mind thought the poem was about. A good example of what I am attempting to identify here is the 1989 "At the Speed of Wine," an 11 page descriptive vision of drinking in a New York City bar with Hart Crane. I got the idea for writing such a poem by reflecting on my co-translation of Vladimir Holan's magnificent "A Night with Hamlet" in which the speaker (Holan) imaginatively engages a special night visitor (a phantasmagoric one-armed crazed Hamlet who appears to the poet in his Prague apartment). My poem is also shadowed by Ulysses' conversation with Tiresias in Book XIII of *The Odyssey.* I mention these influences as background stimulation; I don't think most readers would read my poem and think of Holan or Homer.

Anyway, there is only one draft for "At the Speed of Wine." I sat down after a nice dinner with some good red wine and wrote the poem in about three hours without stopping. I showed it to Caryl the next morning who "edited" it. She eliminated a few repetitions and clarified some images, thus sharpening the focus without doing much rewriting.

I can't compose like that anymore. Maybe all poets have an arsenal which is a combination of the given and the developed and which finally feels almost cleaned out. I say "almost" because as I approached what felt like an emptying in 2012–2014 I moved into a kind of summational "old age" voicing in which I attempted to wrest from my situation material that could be thought of as imagined while standing in my own smoking gate.

**SK:** *"At the Speed of Wine" is a rather astonishing precipitate of three hours writing! Set beside "An Anatomy of the Night" it does demonstrate a certain internalization and condensation of its wide-ranging materials: the dialogue with Crane compacting engagements with Holan, Homer, Hamlet, Artaud, Van Gogh, Caravaggio, etc. In the later work, following some of the language we've been using, the materials are con-stellated more loosely, though no less pointedly. Perhaps this is consistent with a kind of "late style."*

*There's a line in "At the Speed of Wine" that stands out for me in this context: "The book is always late; the book is, in fact, belatedness." You've been writing poetry for more than fifty years, translating poetry that reaches back to the beginnings of modern verse, and writing through the visual arts, including most significantly your writing on the painted caves, that, in your phrase for* Juniper Fuse, *"includes the earliest nights and days of soul-making." I'm wondering how you think of time in your writing — in the act of writing but also in the process of editing your poetry and books of poetry. For example, some of your poems carry indications of dates and places related, presumably, to their composition, others do not. Is poetry bound to the moment in which it is written or does it have some other relationship to time?*

**CE:** The appearance, in 1963, of Yorunomado, birthed out of my gut in seppuku, was my initial thrust into sacramental existence. It was also a furtive attempt to recover what might be called Great Time, or mythic time, not only a break with profane duration but the attempt to engage the paradisiac, primordial situation: time without a past.

However, most of my early writing, given the thoughtlessness in my adolescence and initial manhood, was involved with my own personal history. Here I am thinking of such pieces as "Letter to César Calvo," "Hand," "Sunday Afternoon," "The Bridge at the Mayan Pass," "Still-life with Fraternity" and "Tomb of Donald Duck." Today I am uncomfortable with all of those pieces but I included them in *The Essential Poetry* because they at show me attempting to realize my own provincial, family history.

The poems I have written on Western art and Western artists seem to me today to be a mix of striving in time and release into some of the aspects of Great Time e.g., "Soutine's Lapis" is on one level very engrossed with

Chaim Soutine's painting the stinking hanging fowl he secured from Paris slaughterhouses and the extraordinary otherworldly creatures he turned them into on some of his canvases. On one level, regardless of the subject matter, artistic creation (including poetry) evokes, regardless of the subject (or in the case of a Pollock, the non-subject), the attempt to overcome time. Relative to creation, publication (and exhibition) is always belated, though I guess one could argue that at the very point the poem or painting is completed, it becomes belated to the creative act itself.

As you note in your most appropriate question here, the discovery of the Ice Age painted caves of southwestern France, in the spring of 1974, was huge and very lucky for me, for suddenly I was confronted with an art that had no accessible historical basis including any access to the language of the makers. And to call it "art" is tricky, for surely it is imbedded with utilitarian, magical, and occult prototypes that, primitive art aside, historical art has for the most part never engaged. As someone considerably concerned with my own background I was suddenly faced with a making, the context of which was nearly completely inaccessible. And to put it this way is not to complain! It was the biggest gift in my life, for it put me in touch with a genuine back wall, the earliest days and nights of soul-making. And that feeling of having been put in contact with something that might be called the origin of art was extraordinarily encouraging and gave me the sense that I could possibly be part of something beyond what modern poetry with at best a hazy sense of a Greek "back wall" had envisioned.

**SK:** *Does this engagement with the paradisiac, primordial situation — time without a past — figure in your creative practice as a translator or in your prose writing?*

**CE:** As for poets who I have translated: Aimé Césaire's poetry in the 1948 *Solar Throat Slashed* is permeated by elements of a cosmological myth, involving a self-immolating solar divinity who generates the processes of destruction and renewal. As the speaker says in the powerful "At the Locks of the Void,"

It is I who sing with a voice still caught up in the bab-
bling of elements. It is sweet to be a piece of wood a cork
a drop of water in the torrential waters of the end and of
the new beginning. It is sweet to doze off in the shattered
heart of things.

Or in the same poem:

I await the boiling. I await the baptism of sperm. I
await the wingbeat of the great seminal albatross supposed
to make a new man of me. I await the immense tap, the
vertiginous slap that shall consecrate me as a knight of a
plutonian order. I await in the depths of my pores the sa-
cred intrusion of the benediction.

While Antonin Artaud cannot be called a shaman proper, there is a
shamanic resemblance binding his life and work. When I hold up Artaud's
image, I see shamanic elements in it, like a black root-work suspended, co-
agulated yet unstable, in liquid. For example, while in the asylum of Rodez
in 1945–46, he bore, out of his heart, a new progeny of warrior-daughters
who became his assaulted messengers and saviors. He used the block of
wood that Dr. Delmas placed in his room like a drum. He also had a
"bridge" which he wrote was located between his anus and sex, and it was
upon that bridge that he claimed he was murdered by God who pounced
on him in order to sack his poetry. Spitting and a falsetto voice were also
present. Of course what is missing in such a shamanic scenario is a com-
munity. Artaud is a Kafka man, put through a profound and transfiguring
ritual while finding out, stage by stage, that it no longer counts. He is a
shaman in a nightmare in which all the supporting input from a community
that appreciates the shaman's death and transformation as an aspect of its
own wholeness is, instead, handed over to mockers who revile the novice
at each stage of his initiation.

Juniper Fuse is of course my attempt to link poetry to what may be its
origin, or back wall, in the some two dozen or so hybrid figures to be found
in Upper Paleolithic cave imagery. Since over half of the writing in this
book is in prose, or prose poetry, such would constitute a positive response

to your question. I think that some of the strongest support for such think-ing is to be found in the 5-part "Cosmogonic Collage" that concludes the book. Section One, "The Dive," examines a myth that several scholars have proposed can be traced back to the last Ice Age. I link a shaman-creator diving to the bottom of the sea as an animal or bird in order to bring up creational material to a Cro-Magnon artist descending to the depths of a cave and mixing cave water with red ochre or black manganese to draw animals on stone walls, very ancient indications of what we today call the creative act. In Section Two I describe what I call a Black Goddess stone tree only partially emerged from stalactites, fissures and folds. Possibly as early as 25,000 B.P. Cro-Magnon people identified and marked this proto-World Tree. And in Section Five, I describe a forked blade from Le Placard dated roughly between 18,000 and 16,000 B.P. that has a woman's groin carved in the base that appears to be projecting an ithyphallic blade. To put it idiomatically, this is a *hole that grows into a pole*. These three examples strike me as some of the most unique and cogent examples of very early imaginal workings of time without a past.

**SK:** *These are extremely potent examples of this problematic. However in posing the question I was wondering more specifically about the act of translation or the act of writing prose, as to whether or not you could access this primordial experience through translation or through writing prose, or if, on the other hand, translation and prose writing function in distinct ways for you in terms of your creative practice.*

**CE:** In my response to your 5th question I commented on my approach to translation via time spent with Cid Corman in Kyoto in the early 1960s. While translating writers like Vallejo, Artaud, and Césaire is a challenging linguistic adventure and the deepest way I know of to read them, since I do not take creative liberties in this work I don't think my practice engages anything like primordial experience. I think the closest thing to imaginal depth in this case would be some poems I have written off Artaud in which his mind stirred my mind in one example to engage what I called "black paradise."

That poem is in *Anticline*.

I included only a few prose poems in the *Essential Poetry* now under production at Black Widow because most of them do not show me at my best. The prose I am most satisfied with involves pieces on writers or painters I admire (Paul Blackburn, Gary Snyder, Charles Olson, Artaud, Leon Golub, Chaim Soutine, Paul Celan, Allen Ginsberg, Ron Padgett, Judith Scott, Nancy Spero, and Hart Crane, for example) or on aspects of Upper Paleolithic cave art (which of course unlike writing on contemporary poets drops me into the abyss of origins and Great Time). Some of the prose on Blackburn, Soutine and Crane engages creative imagination (in contrast to critically examining what a particular author has written). The Olson dream presented on p. 262 of *Juniper Fuse* portrays the poet passing from personal consciousness into collective consciousness or the realm of creature souls.

It occurs to me that some of the Horrah Pornoff "Homuncula" workings, in exploring an invented mind, might be thought of as spontaneous creations with an invented temporal duration, though they of course are presented as poems.

Perhaps you have something in mind here that I have not picked up. If so, please write about this and I will try to respond.

**SK:** *This gets to the notion I had in mind — essentially about the difference between writing poetry and translating poetry in your creative life. In my own experience as a translator, the confrontation with the text of another, across the chasms of time, place and cultural context, has often been quite a challenging and humbling psychological experience, akin to being lost in a forest. We've already spoken of your early struggles to bring Vallejo's voice in particular over into English. We didn't mention the fact that the process was ongoing, after your initial publications of his work in the late 1960s, through several new versions of the work, culminating in the publication of the* Complete Poetry *in 2007. You're involved in a similar exercise now with Aimé Césaire's poetry, which you've also been translating since the mid-1960s. Do you get closer to the core of the text with each subsequent translation? Do you find that there any certainties in translation?*

**CE:** In regard to the first part of your question concerning getting closer to the core of a text: over a period of thirty-nine years (1968–2007), I completed three published versions of César Vallejo's *Human Poems,* his most substantial collection. During this period, while writing my own poetry on a nearly daily basis, and editing two literary magazines (for a total of twenty-four years), I became an increasingly focused writer. I think that each new version I did of this Vallejo book became more accurate and precise than earlier ones, and if this is so, the reasons for such involve not only my own growth as a writer, my increasing familiarity with Vallejo's psyche and the Spanish language, but my improved agility to process the help I received from two co-translators (Octavio Corvalan with Vallejo's Spanish Civil War poems and José Rubia Barcia with the *Human Poems*) along with the half dozen other people who made useful suggestions to my versions that we went over together.

Other than a little collection of early Aimé Césaire poems I translated with my old friend Denis Kelly in Bloomington, 1966, I have again had two splendid co-translators with my ongoing attention to his writing: Annette Smith who I worked with off and on for a decade (our collaboration producing translations of the 1956 *Notebook of a Return to the Native Land, The Collected Poetry of Aimé Césaire,* and *Lyric & Narrative Poetry 1946–1982*) and A. James Arnold who I began to work with around 2008. Arnold and I have published two Césaire collections (*Solar Throat Slashed* and *The Original 1939 Notebook of a Return to the Native Land*), and have recently completed a version of *The Complete Poetry of Aimé Césaire* which Wesleyan University Press will publish in 2017. While I still respect Annette's and my Césaire work I have become a better translator than when I worked with her in the 1980s and James Arnold is the leading Césaire scholar most probably in the world. Thus it has made sense for Arnold and I to retranslate the earlier Eshleman/Smith versions as well as the rest of Césaire's poetry.

It is also important to note that I began to translate Vallejo during my poetic apprenticeship, and I often worked on him in Kyoto when I was lost or blocked with my own poems. By the time I began to work on Césaire, I had fifteen years with Vallejo under my belt and a pretty good sense of what I wanted to accomplish in my own poetry.

As for certainties in translation: That is a slippery question! One reason that I have worked with co-translators is that as a translator-poet I have had to undermine my impulse to embellish or simply alter the original when it seemed flat or, especially in Vallejo's case, when it was densely ambiguous. Working with the people I mention above has brought me as close to certainty as I could come. When one is translating a living author who is available for questioning (I made three trips to Paris to ask Césaire questions about arcane and coined words in the early 1980s), the chances of certainty in the work theoretically improve. However, here I must acknowledge that when I was translating the poetry of Michel Deguy, with Deguy, daily, in Paris in the early 1980s, I discovered that from time to time he would make up a meaning for a word we were discussing that, were I to accept it, would appear simply as a mistranslation! So maybe it is better here to say that while a translator can court certainty he can never fall asleep with complete satisfaction in her arms.

**SK:** *Working with these co-translators to bring the voices of other poets into the reservoirs of English suggests a kind of creative community at work that seems to transcend any kind of "anxiety of influence" in Harold Bloom's sense of that phrase. The notion also evokes for me the dedication of* The Price of Experience *to Robert Kelly and Jerome Rothenberg, as "fellow Argonauts," which I take to suggest reference to a creative community among you. Aside from the co-translators you've mentioned, who have been your closest collaborators?*

**CE:** While I do not think you could call her a collaborator in the sense that we wrote poems together, Caryl, my wife, who edited my work from roughly 1973 to 2008, is the closest to a collaborator. I acknowledge her work at the beginning of the 72 pages of notes that end *The Essential Poetry*. I would show Caryl drafts of poems and she would make comments that often led to rewriting or rethinking particular moves. All in all, she sharpened my focus and caught a number of clichés and repetitions. What I have been able to accomplish as a poet is profoundly in debt to her.

In 1996 I sent a copy of *Nora's Roar* to Adrienne Rich who I had not had any contact with for decades (I had a brief acquaintance with her in NYC in the late 1960s but lost contact with her in the early 1970s after her husband committed suicide and she became a lesbian who for some years had little or no contact with men). I got a wonderful letter from her after she read my elegy for Nora (who had been one of her oldest friends), and this started up a regular correspondence that ended a few weeks before Adrienne's death in 2012. We must have exchanged around 300 letters and many of them contain, on both our parts, poems in progress that the other poet would comment on. Adrienne had a very sharp eye and her criticisms of my work mainly entailed objections to what she felt were rhetorical flourishes. I suspect in this regard she helped me more than I helped her as the poems she sent me I think had already been through some revision.

Several author friends have made useful comments on aspects of my work: Cid Corman on early Vallejo versions in Kyoto; Paul Blackburn on some poems in the late 1960s, and Ron Padgett, whose recent comments on drafts of *An Anatomy of the Night* and "Velmar's Lemon" (still unpublished) were extremely useful in helping me to finish this work.

I should also acknowledge your comments on certain poems to include in *The Essential Poetry* that I had, at the time you wrote me, left out of this evolving manuscript. I reread the poems you listed and put some of them in.

But in terms of real collaboration, a one-to-one writing relationship, I think I have only experienced this with Annette Smith, José Rubia Barcia, and James Arnold in Césaire and Vallejo translating.

I referred to Robert Kelly and Jerome Rothenberg as "fellow Argonauts" because we have been friends in poetry and in our personal lives since the early 1960s. And also because I feel that our three bodies of work is one of the most original and accomplished artistic contributions of our generation. The territory that our three bodies of work covers is, in my opinion, spectacular. I feel that the three of us have continued to push on and out, beyond those who influenced us, into the previously uncharted.

SK: *That push, on and out, as you say, beyond your — and Kelly's and Rothenberg's — influences, itself strikes me as a defining, even constitutive element of all three bodies of work, and of others' besides, but of your moment, if that word can be allowed, in poetry and really in thought and ethics as well. There's this engagement with language and life in the work that is personal and historical, psychological and cultural, and profoundly restless and searching, probing. For all the politically correct lip service to "diversity" in contemporary writing, my sense is that that search, that push on and out, has become all too rare in poetry today. Perhaps I am missing something, but I am reminded of the beginning of the foreword Adrienne Rich wrote for your book* Companion Spider, *where she wrote:"There is very little around today... that possesses the depth and substance of this book... the accumulated prose-work of a poet and translator who has gone more deeply into his art, its process and demands, than any modern American poet since Robert Duncan or Muriel Rukeyser." It's a marvelous encomium, of course but also true. Perhaps poetry as the scholar's art (Wallace Stevens' remark that you have quoted at times) seems out of fashion today. Do you share this sense of contemporary poetry? Are you aware of poets today whose writing continues this approach to poetry?*

**CE:** If Paul Hoover's *Postmodern American Poetry* (the second edition, 2013) is representative of the new, I would say that the university degree writing programs have had a very detrimental effect on a number of aspects of poetry as I know and respect it. Flarf is simply mediocre writing and Conceptualism is aestheticized plagiarism. As I have mentioned or at least implied earlier in our interview, I do not think one learns how to become a poet in a degree writing workshop where one spends most of one's attention listening to the opinions of other students who are also, at best, novices. Academically speaking, I think one builds up one's literary arsenal by discovering for oneself, on one's own, the essential American poets to study, of the past and of one's own generation and then by reading all of their writing. Such research must be amplified by learning reading skills in at least one foreign language along with reading some of the poets of that language in the original, and reading translations of them, with the aim of teaching oneself how to critique translations.

I should add that besides Robert Kelly and Jerome Rothenberg, I think that Michael McClure, Rachel Blau DuPlessis, Andrew Joron, Rae Armantrout, Will Alexander, John Olson, and Sarah Fox (to name the poets who first come to mind) are doing genuinely innovative writing today.

As for the Wallace Steven's statement on poetry as the scholar's art (from his book *Adagia*), I understand it to mean two possible things: that poetry may be the art that appeals most to scholars, and that poets can incorporate scholarly research without lessening the intuitive drive it takes to write commanding poetry. Basho, André Breton, Octavio Paz, and José

Lezama Lima are four non-American poets who come to mind here. I think of translation as on one level scholarly activity, and I think one can make a similar case for editing a literary journal.

**SK:** *Do you think that the digital revolution (the internet but also digital printing) has had any meaningful impact on the ways that poetry is written and read today? Have "little" magazines, broadsides and chapbooks been replaced by digital forms of publication?*

**CE:** There is a curious comparable increase in graduate degree writing programs and internet blogs and e-zines. I don't have any exact figures here but one explanation for this double increase may be the following: an e-zine is much easier to set up and to operate than, say, a magazine like *Sulfur* which cost near the end of its run in 2000, around $6000 per issue to produce, pay contributors, and mail, with roughly 800 subscribers. Over the magazine's 18-year run, we had various distributors, none of which really made any money for the magazine (and one, Truck, when it went bankrupt owed the magazine $2400 none of which we ever received). *Jacket,* an e-zine from Australia, other than the cost of computer equipment and monthly server fees, had no other costs that I am aware of, and must be read by thousands of people online. I once submitted to *Jacket* a trilogue with Paul Hoover and Maxine Chernoff about the various magazines the three of us had edited, and it appeared the next day. Thus for young writers with Masters or PHD Degrees in creative writing it is much, much simpler, and inexpensive, to start up a e-zine or blog than a 250-page magazine like *Sulfur.*

While I imagine that an e-zine with *Sulfur*'s range and depth could be produced, I am not aware of any. Nor am I aware of any print magazines today that can be compared to *Sulfur.*

You ask if the digital revolution has had any impact on the way that poetry is written today. Hard to really tell, but I suspect that given its tie-in with the degree writing programs it has. Both Flarf and Conceptual Poetry are primarily 21st century phenomena, along with other cyberpoetries. And I must acknowledge that were I a senior at Indiana University today, knowing no more than I knew then, I might be tempted to enroll in an Masters or PHD creative writing program. Thus educating myself on my own, with a lot of books and a few correspondents (and getting out of USA to experience the foreign cultures of Mexico, Japan, and Peru) can be seen as my response to the young writer's situation in my era.

On the other hand, for all I know (since at eighty I have moreorless stopped reading first collections of poetry and hardly read any magazines online or off) there may be young writers out there doing what I did in the late 1950s. From time to time a young poet who does not appear to be in a writing degree program, sends me some poems to read. Some of them are genuinely interesting. The poets I mentioned in the last post as doing innovative writing today, while for the most part several generations younger than me, came into poetry in the non-digital world.

**SK:** *Can you say a little bit about what you mean by the word "negation" in the last paragraph of the essay "An Alchemist with One Eye on Fire" where you wrote: "I continue to regard poetry as a form in which the realities of the spirit can be tested by critical intelligence, a form in which the blackness of the heart of man can be confronted, in which affirmation is only viable when it survives repeated immersions in negation — in short, a form that can be made responsible for all that the poet knows about himself as his world."*

**CE:** My comment on "negation" is derived from a statement by Paul Tillich: "A life process is the more powerful, the more non-being it can include in its self-affirmation without being destroyed by it." As well as from the Kafka quotation I mentioned earlier. In contrast to the kind of research I did on Ice Age cave imagery which I thought of as affirming the oldest creative core of humankind, a civil or political focus turns the writer into a kind of moving target in evasion of those forces society uses to disarticulate him: self-censorship as well as editorial censorship: the shying away from materials that disturb a predictable and aesthetically-acceptable response.

In my poem "The Assault," I wanted to get the possible government conspiracy on 9/11 into the poetic record. I seek to build an atmosphere of political awareness into much of what I write—to write a civil poetry as a citizen-writer. I want a sense of my own times, on a national/international register, to permeate my language. It would be simplistic to claim that all political material is negative. However positive political acts do not call out to me to be addressed in poetry. I use the word "civil" here to complex the word "political" and to remove from my use of it the agit-prop implications attached to traditional political poetry. In my writing, I want to protect an imaginative openness to spontaneity and free-association in image choice. If I am going to use a politician in a poem, I have to figure out ways to imagine him and absorb him into my sensibility. This is close to thinking of him as a text to be translated.

Over the years, I have written a number of poems testing my sense of the negative political, such as "Basra Highway" (the American invasion of Iraq), "Hardball" (the LA police beating of Rodney King), "El Mozote" (the massacre of some eight hundred villagers by the American government-supported Salvadoran Army), "Minor Drag" (a poem proposing that the 9/11 destruction of the three towers involved a controlled demolition), and "Monumental" (a tribute to my dear friend, the political-activist painter, Leon Golub).

In the fall of 2004, Caryl & I spent a month at the Rockefeller Study Center on Lake Como, Italy, where I daily studied a large reproduction of Hieronymus Bosch's triptych, *The Garden of Earthly Delights*. My 60-page improvisation on the triptych, in poetry and prose, tips it, at points, into the 21st century so that, for example, the American assault on Fallujah is there as a disaster in Bosch's Apocalypse. In one section, I sense the presence of Bush and Rumsfeld in the apocalyptic mayhem to be found in Bosch's right-hand panel:

> The intoxications of immortality light up the switchboards when
> someone is murdered.
> The furnaces of immortality are fed with the bodies of people who
> look a little different than us.
> How does this work, Donald Rumsfeld?
> Does your Reaper retreat an inch for each sixteen-year-old Iraqi boy
> snipered while out looking for food?
> Men with political power are living pyramids of slaughtered others.
> Bush is a Babelesque pyramid of blood-scummed steps.
> The discrepancy
> between the literal suit and psychic veracity is nasty to contemplate.
> Imagine a flea with a howitzer shadow
> or a worm whose shade is a nuclear blaze.

***

This interview with Stuart Kendall was published in the March 2016 online edition of *Rain Taxi* magazine. Stuart Kendall is a writer, editor, & translator working at the intersection of poetics, visual culture, & design. His books include *Gilgamesh, Georges Bataille, The End of Art and Design,* and a number of other edited or translated volumes. Black Widow Press published his edited volume, *Clayton Eshleman: The Whole Art,* in 2014. Kendall lives with his family in Oakland, California, where he teaches at the California College of the Arts.

# NOTES

"For Connie Culp": Ms. Culp (1963–) is the first United States recipient of a face transplant, performed at the Cleveland Clinic in December 2008. She had been shot in the face with a 12-gauge shotgun by her husband. Surgeon Maria Siemionow led a team of eight doctors in a 22 hour operation which replaced 80% of Culp's face with that of Anna Kaspar's, her donor.

"Mandalizing": "Anne" is Anne Waldman. The quotations from Jung are from Volumes 12 and 18 of his *Collected Works*. The James Hillman material is from the "Praxis" section in *The Dream and the Underworld*. Material on mandalas in the poem is also from *Mandala / Sacred Circles in Tibetan Buddhism*, "Eight great charnel grounds" from Rigpa Wiki (available online) and *Chakrasamvara (Buddhist Deity)* available via www.himalayanart.org/image.cfm/ 86435.html. The Michael Parenti material is from his online political archive, specifically *Friendly Feudalism: The Tibet Myth, 2007*.

Waldman published her edited sections of my letter to her that begins this poem in Book III, XXV of *The Iovis Trilogy*.

"For My Niece Liana": See "The Dive" in *Juniper Fuse* for information on the oldest myth.

"Hovering Lara Glenum": Glenum is the author of several books of poetry, including *The Hounds of No* (2005), *Maximum Gaga* (2008) & *Pop Corpse* (2013). She teaches at Louisiana State University in Baton Rouge LA.

"For Ken Mikolowski": Mikolowski, with his late wife Ann, founded The Alternative Press in the 1960s, which published local & national poets for some 30 years. He is the author of *Little Mysteries* (1979), *Big Enigmas* (1991), & *That That* (2015). He now lives on a lake near Dexter, MI.

"For Don Mee Choi": Choi was born in South Korea & came to the U.S. via Hong Kong. She lives in Seattle. She is the author of *The Morning News Is Exciting* (2010) & *Hardly War* (2015). She is also the translator of Ch'oe Sŭng-ja, Kim Hyesoon & Yi Yŏn-ju.

"A Half Hour with Basquiat": Jean-Michel Basquiat (1960–1988) was born in Brooklyn & died in NoHo, NYC. He began as an obscure graffiti artist in NYC and evolved into an acclaimed Neo-Expressionist and Primitivist painter.

"For Joyelle McSweeney" Along with her husband Johannes Goransson, Joyelle is the founder of Action Books. She is the author of several collections of poetry, including *Percussion Grenade* (2012) & *Salamander* (2013). She lives in South Bend, IN.

"Self As Selva": The Northrop Frye quotations are from *Words with Power / Being A Second Study of The Bible and Literature*.

"The Eye Mazes of Unica Zürn": For Unica Zürn drawings, see *Unica Zürn / Bilder 1953–1970,* Verlag Brinkmann und Bose, Berlin. A more recent compilation is *Unica Zürn,* Halle Saint-Pierre, Paris. Kokodera (Moss Temple) is in Kyoto, Japan. In my *Reciprocal Distillations, Archaic Design,* & *Anticline* there are other poems on Zürn & her art.

"While Drinking Coffee at Zingerman's": "Rebecca Kamate" is not the woman's real name. Her rape is recounted by Adam Hochchild in his August 13, 2009 article "Rape in the Congo," NYRB. Kevin Davis' poem "Lateral Argument" is in his 2008 book *The Golden Age of Paraphernalia.*

"Stitt Horns In": The Hillman quotation is from "Beyond Interiorization" in *Animal Presences.*

"North Tower Exploding": My other two poems on the 9/11 assault (more appropriately referred to as "The Pentagon Three Towers Bombing") may be found in *CE / The Essential Poetry 1960–2015.* They are "The Assault" & "Minor Drag." See also the passage in "Wound Interrogation" in this collection that addresses this assault.

"A Morning Writhing with Revelation": The Hillman quotation is from "Psychic Beauty" in *Blue Fire.* I highly recommend Michael Peppiatt's *Francis Bacon: Anatomy of an Enigma.*

"I have been shut down four months now…": In 2010 & 2011 Caryl Eshleman suffered several spontaneous vertebral fractures due to, we later found out, osteoporosis. During 2010 especially there were complications (such as height & weight loss associated with the kyphoplasty-sealed fractures) that were mysterious & unnerving. As I write this note in June 2014, Caryl has still not fully recovered. "Lascaux is now so wounded…": In the early part of 2000, articles appeared in *The Wall Street Journal, Time,* & *Archeology* magazines reporting serious mold & fungus deterioration in many of the paintings & engravings of the famous Lascaux cave in the French Dordogne. Up through 2009 a website www.savelascaux.org presented this situation as being alarming, with some of the commentators, such as the British archeologist Paul Bahn, writing that those in charge of the cave had "orchestrated a policy of misinformation, denial, and blame-shifting since the beginning of the crisis in 2000." I got in touch with my old friend, the French rock art expert Jean Clottes, to find out how he evaluated the Lascaux situation. According to Clottes, a symposium on the cave, held in 2009, reported that 14 of the engravings & paintings had black stains. Given the fact that there are over 600 paintings & 1500 engravings in the cave, this indicates a serious but not catastrophic situation. According to Clottes, the articles on the cave mentioned above, as well as the website, & Paul Bahn, had irresponsibly exaggerated the deterioration. Before contacting Clottes, I wrote an article on what appeared to be the dreadful situation at Lascaux, called "Lascaux, Lost Caul," which appeared, with photos, on the Cerise blog, & on Pierre Joris's Nomadics blog. Having not visited the cave since 1997, I can only pray that Clottes is right. A 2012 article in his *International Newsletter on Rock Art*, "Lascaux: Back to Balance," by the journalist Pedro Lima, supports Clottes' viewpoint.

In March, 2014, Clottes wrote me: "About Lascaux: I'm glad to say there is nothing new i.e., the cave is at rest, as it should be. A major project of a big replica (Lascaux 4) is underway. Should be finished in a couple of years. The Chauvet replica should be inaugurated within 14 months. It will be a major achievement."

"Cecilia Vicuña Thread": The poem was evoked by *Drawing Papers 34 / DIS SOLVING threads of water and light* by César Paternosto and Cecilia Vicuña.

"Black Jaguar": This poem draws on visions from Kenneth A. Symington's translation of César Calvo's book, *The Three Halves of Ino Moxo.*

"Mezcal": The material for this poem is taken from the August 2010, Numero 98, issue of *Artes de Mexico.*

"*Some Lady*": This portrait of Adele Bloch-Bauer, the wife of a wealthy Viennese industrialist, was painted by Gustaf Klimt in 1912. It is part of the permanent collection of the Neue Gallerie in NYC.

"*Wound Interrogation*": This 1948 painting by Matta is in the Chicago Art Institute and reproductions of it can be accessed online. Paul Valery's "response to the final disease" may be found in Michael Moore's translation of Guido Ceronetti's *The Silence of the Body.*

"*Tree Roots and Trunks*": There is a fine double-page color reproduction of this painting by van Gogh in *Van Gogh in Auvers / His Last Days*. The painting is not dated, though it was certainly painted in July, 1890; Van Gogh is reported to have shot himself on July 26, 1890. Chances are the current title was added by someone after his death three days later.

"Michaux's Signs": The opening quotation is from *Drawing Papers 14 / Emergences / Resurgences,* by Henri Michaux & translated by Richard Sieburth. Several other Michaux quotations in the poem are from my & Bernard Bador's translation of Michaux's poem "Movements" published in my *The Price of Experience*. The McClure "animal sounds" are from Michael's book *Ghost Tantras.*

"Bodhisattva Remains": This poem is based on an installation of five pairs of hanging paper scrolls called *FULL LOTUS: Bodhisattvas at Ayutthaya* by the painter Mary Heebner. Each scroll has a large snapshot of one of the brutalized sculptures.

"Stevens at Tenochtitlan": The John Lash quotation is from Lash's monogram, *Twins and the double.* The Weston La Barre comments on what he calls an "archosis" are to be found in *Muelos: A Stone Age Superstitiion About Sexuality.* The Tenochtitlan information is from a range of sources.

"Les Eyzies, June 2008": Some thirty-five years ago I discovered my true home while living outside the town of Les Eyzies de Tayac in the French Dordogne. This reversal of background occurred through my discovery of the origin of image making in the Upper Paleolithic painted caves in the Dordogne, Lot, and Ariège regions. While leading what has turned out to be Caryl's & my last cave tour to some of these caves, I realized that this would be my last visit to this realm that had come to mean so much to me. Homage to Nancee Clark, our cave tour director from the Ringling School of Art and Design in Sarasota, Florida, & to Mathilde Sitbon, our travel coordinator in France.

"The Jointure": The word "kelson" comes from the 5th section of Walt Whitman's 1855 version of "Song of Myself," where he writes: "that a kelson of the creation is love." *Webster's International Dictionary* defines the word as a shipbuilding term: "a longitudinal structure incorporated with the framing of a ship to contribute stiffness, prevent local deformation, and distribute over a considerable length the effects of concentrated loads."

As in the past, I have drawn assorted words and materials from the Baby's Book of Events my parents kept for me during the first two years of my life.

For information on Asmat adolescent sexual initiation, see the "Ethnographic: Old World" chapter in La Barre's previously-cited *Muelos*. There are photographs of & commentary on the Asmat "tjemen" in *The Asmat of New Guinea: The Michael C. Rockefeller Expedition 1961*.

For detailed information on Xochipilli, visit "Erowid Entheogen Vaults: Xochipilli" online.

For more information on "the Cosmic Dive" see "The Dive" section in *Juniper Fuse: Upper Paleolithic Imagination & the Construction of the Underworld*.

In section 13 of the poem, "Dicht" and its analogs comes from the "Dream Material" section of Hillman's *The Dream and the Underworld*. The Hillman quotation beginning "Each dream is a child of Night" is from "The Brood of Night" section of the same book.

The Gilgamesh material is based on my reading of a new translation of the poem by Stuart Kendall, published by Contra Mundum in 2012.

"Nested Dolls": I am convinced that the statement "Image is the reality of the invisible world" comes from José Lezama Lima's writings and that I have it somewhere in my papers. Having not been able to locate it for this note, I offer the reader the following paragraph from Lezama Lima's essay "Confluences," translated by James Irby and published in *Sulfur* #25 and *A Sulfur Anthology* (Wesleyan U Press, 2015):

> When potency is applied to a point or when it acts in space, it does so always in company with the imago, the deepest unity we can know between the realm of the stars and the earth. If potency were to act without the imago, it would be only a self-destructive act having no participation, but every act, every potency is an infinite growth, an overriding excess, in which the stars reinforce momentary visibility, which, without the image as the only recourse available to man, would be an impenetrable excess. In that way, man takes over that excess, makes it come forth and reincorporates a new excess. All poesis is an act of participation in that excess, a participation of man in the universal spirit, in the Holy Spirit, in the universal mother.

"The Dream's Navel": My awareness of *kundalini* and The Muladhara Chakra dates back to a startling experience I had near the end of Reichian-oriented therapy with Dr. Sidney Handelman in NYC in 1969. I describe this experience in "Interface II: 'Fracture'" to be found in *Juniper Fuse*.

\* \* \*

# AT EIGHTY-ONE

I just awoke from a dream of being in Vienna with Caryl & Wilhelm
    Reich.
We were at an institute & Reich, late at night, asked me to go out and
    get him a cigar.
I walked out to the river! Autumn evening light, the river glistening,
beautiful beyond language—or was the river language?

Think of this page as a lighthouse beam on night's cornucopian density
thousand-wired to the boles & excrescences that have inspired me:

    Bud Powell's midnight fulgurations on "Tea for Two"
    César Vallejo imprisoning me in global life
    The centroversion of Lascaux
    Hieronymus Bosch vibrating wizard-cruciform insight

Side by side with Caryl in that liminal zone between home &
poetry's jaguar mouth. I stared for 25 years into a cave womb
where a bison-headed Cro-Magnon hunter danced after an equally
    hybrid herd.
In the Les Trois Frères engraving I spotted a long-haired young woman
seated inside the hunter's lower body & noted:
"the hybrid is the engine of anima display"


    \*


Why don't you risk weather-roping a raft to the stain of being eighty-
    one?
The pattern guide is oblivion spell, words no longer safe from sleep's
    connect to being gone—
I'm wondering how Pollock would have "dripped" 3:19 AM
when & if the spell of vanish had lifted the octopus out of modes of
    knowing—
to write now in the flow of no, use "no",
scratch your "are" as if in Combarelles,   be first as you last,

bolster, game the maze of no longer parsing what from whether,
is it not time to forget the broken pylons of your strife gain,
now the problem of saying is moles gnawing through each word
since no word instills a savior path.

            *


The mesh of now & the life-force we undermined in Eden:
a crucible clouded with the frailty of forever...

Beautiful river also an open skull emitting Trump & nebular gas...

Let's go shop, feel the sunny autumn breeze
in the randomness of fixture as a tuned spar.

All adds in as nothing floods out
& nothing

adds up
as all.

        November, 2016

CLAYTON ESHLEMAN was born in Indianapolis, Indiana, June 1, 1935. He has a B.A. in Philosophy and an M.A.T. in English Literature from Indiana University. He has lived in Mexico, Japan, Taiwan, Korea, Peru, France, Czechoslovakia, and Hungary. He is presently Professor Emeritus, English Department, Eastern Michigan University. Since 1986 he has lived in Ypsilanti, Michigan with his wife Caryl who over the past forty years has been the primary reader and editor of his poetry and prose. His first collection of poetry, *Mexico & North,* was published in Kyoto, Japan in 1962.

Photo credit: Tom Wallace

From 1968 to 2004, Black Sparrow Press brought out thirteen collection of his poetry. In 2006, Black Widow Press became his main publisher and with *The Price of Experience* (2012) had brought out seven collections of his poetry, prose, and translations, including, in 2008, *The Grindstone of Rapport / A Clayton Eshleman Reader.* Wesleyan University Press has also published six of his books, including *Juniper Fuse: Upper Paleolithic Imagination & the Construction of the Underworld* (2003), the first study of Ice Age cave art by a poet. Eshleman has published sixteen collections of translations, including *Watchfiends & Rack Screams* by Antonin Artaud (Exact Change, 1995), *The Complete Poetry of César Vallejo* with a Foreword by Mario Vargas Llosa (University of California Press, 2007), and *Aimé Césaire: The Collected Poetry* (co-translated with Annette Smith, University of California Press, 1983).

Clayton also founded and edited two of the most innovative poetry journals of the later part of the 20th century: *Caterpillar* (20 issues, 1967–1973) and *Sulfur* (46 issues, 1981–2000). Doubleday-Anchor published *A Caterpillar Anthology* in 1971 and Wesleyan in November 2015 published a 700-page *Sulfur Anthology.*

Among his recognitions and awards are a Guggenheim Fellowship in Poetry, 1978; The National Book Award in Translation, 1979; two grants from the NEA, 1979, 1981; three grants from the NEH, 1980, 1981, 1988; two Landon Translation Prizes from the Academy of American Poets, 1981, 2008; 13 NEA grants for *Sulfur* magazine, 1983–1996; The Alfonse X. Sabio

Award for Excellence in Translation, San Diego State University, 2002; a Rockefeller Study Center residency in Bellagio, Italy, 2004, and a Hemmingway Translation Grant in 2015.

In 2014 Black Widow Press published *Clayton Eshleman / The Whole Art,* an anthology of essays on Eshleman's work over the decades, edited by Stuart Kendall. In the fall of 2015, Black Widow brought out *Clayton Eshleman / The Essential Poetry 1960–2015* and in 2017 Wesleyan will bring out a 950-page bilingual edition of *The Complete Poetry of Aimé Césaire,* co-translated with A. James Arnold.

His poetry has been featured in both volumes (1994 and 2013) of the *Norton Postmodern American Poetry.*

His website is www.claytoneshleman.com

# TITLES FROM BLACK WIDOW PRESS
## TRANSLATION SERIES

# MODERN POETRY SERIES

# LITERARY THEORY / BIOGRAPHY SERIES

WWW.BLACKWIDOWPRESS.COM